LIFE IN THE SLOW LANE

A Tourbook of Central Ohio for Bicyclists, Time Travelers, and Other Backroads Buffs.

Fifteen backroads tours featuring covered bridges, pioneer cemeteries, Indian memorials, nature preserves, old churches, water mills, and much, much more!

By
JEFF AND NADEAN DI SABATO TRAYLOR

Copyright 1986 by Jeffrey and Nadean DiSabato Traylor

Published and distributed by:
Backroad Chronicles
P.O. Box 292066
Columbus, Ohio 43229

Printed in Columbus, Ohio U.S.A.
ISBN 0-93-591301-7
Third Printing

Cover photo: J. Traylor
Green's Heritage Museum, Loop #6

Introduction

This guidebook was written for modern day adventurers who wish to travel the backroads to Central Ohio's past and discover a world that lies beyond the freeways and city lights. Whether you are a bicyclist, birdwatcher, history buff, or simply like to roam, you will find many hours of enjoyable and informative touring on these back country roads. Ohio's past becomes present as you discover covered bridges, Indian memorials, pioneer cemeteries, water mills, old churches, and other historical points of interest. Our natural heritage likewise is awaiting your exploration in the bogs, kettle lakes, streams and valleys of Central Ohio. To further complement your ramblings, many of the loops also include swimming beaches, campgrounds, picnic tables, and walking trails.

A simple-to-use trip planning guide provides information to help you select your tour, and an Ohio outline map gives you the location of the ride's starting point at a glance. A historical narrative accompanies each loop description, and information about the various points of interest is provided. County road maps have been used as base maps for the tours, and each route is clearly marked and annotated.

If you choose to explore on bicycle, as we did, remember to be careful, obey all traffic laws, and make yourself visible. Exert extra caution in those few instances when it is necessary to cross or travel along the busier state routes. We selected paved roads for the tours, and have indicated on the maps those rare short stretches when the surface becomes dirt or gravel. Of course, road and traffic conditions are subject to change. And finally, know your own skills and physical limits before embarking on your bicycle. If in doubt, see your physician first.

HAPPY TRAILS!

About the Authors

Jeff and Nadean Traylor are devoted explorers of out-of-the-way places. Avid bicyclists, they recently completed a 1,600 mile bike trip through Ohio, Michigan, and Ontario, and found, in Dorothy's words, "there's no place like home". In addition to being chroniclers of country roads, the Traylors established a successful retail business in Columbus' historic North Market, and have been professionally engaged in the fields of mental health and retardation. Both are natives of Central Ohio.

Acknowledgments

The authors wish to thank the following agencies for their assistance in providing information that helped make this book possible:

The Ohio Historical Society

The Ohio Department of Natural Resources

The Ohio Department of Transportation

The Ohio Department of Tourism
1-800-BUCKEYE

For further reading on Ohio's historical and natural heritage, we particularly recommend *The Frontiersmen* by Allan W. Eckert and *Ohio's Natural Heritage,* edited by Michael B. Lafferty.

Trip Planning Guide

# Name	Length (miles)	Historical site	Nature preserve	Museum	Covered bridge	Scenic river	Swimming	Picnic tables	Camping (State Park)	Pioneer cemetery	Hiking/walking trails
1. The Three Sisters	54		X	X	1	X		X	X	X	X
2. Tecumseh and Friend	27	X	X		3	X		X	X	X	X
3. Ice Age Deja Vu	39		X				X	X	X	X	X
4. Mackachack	39	X	X				X	X	X	X	X
5. Prairie Flower	45		X				X	X		X	
6. Stage Coach	44			X			X	X		X	
7. Treaty Line	49	X				X	X	X		X	
8. Old Stone Church	25	X				X					
9. Books of Stone	46				1		X	X	X	X	
10. Slate Run Farm	30		X	X				X	X		X
11. The Logan Elm	29	X						X	X		
12. Glacier's Edge	34		X		1				X		
13. Old Wooden Bridge	49		X		3				X	X	X
14. Arboretum	40		X	X				X		X	X
15. Flint Ridge	20	X	X	X				X			X

Tour Starting Points

To Natalie and Dante

LOOP #1

Distance: 54 miles

Terrain: Gently rolling with a few steep hills

County: Greene

The Three Sisters Ride

  This is one of two rides from John Bryan State Park, providing an opportunity for camping overnight and riding both the Tecumseh and Three Sisters Rides. The Three Sisters Ride follows roads southwestward that may be familiar to cyclists as the Little Miami Bikeway, departing from that route near the quaint little town of Bellbrook, and venturing on to the Sugarcreek Reserve. After a visit with the Three Sisters of Sugarcreek, you'll wind your way back to the park over country lanes, passing by a pioneer church that stands proudly in the open countryside, its steeple rising against the sky. This is a ride rich in natural beauty and pioneer history, although the Three Sisters consider our entire state history as little more than current events.

  King Henry VI was on the throne of England, Joan of Arc had just been burned at the stake, and Queen Isabella of Spain was not yet born, when, in 1432, three acorns fell quietly to the ground on a continent yet unknown to Europe in a land destined to become known as Ohio. The three white oaks were well established when Christopher Columbus set foot in the New World. Hunting parties of Indians seeking buffalo passed beneath the boughs of the Three Sisters, and buffalo herds so large that it took two days for them to pass at thirty abreast created a nearby buffalo "road", which became known centuries later as U.S. 68. The sisters were just entering their prime when the colonists threw off the yoke of British rule, and they must have felt some trepidation with the coming of the pioneers and their land-clearing axes. As their fellows fell to those axes to become cabins, furniture, and gun stocks, the Three Sisters touched fingertips and somehow survived. They saw the rise of Tecumseh and the wars between the Indians and settlers. They watched fugitive slaves running for freedom through these woods along the underground railroad. Recently, they've seen the highways and cars come with the "modern" era. And, incredibly, after more than 550 years, these Three Sisters are still standing at Sugarcreek Reserve, watching us pass beneath their huge branches today.

The trail to the Three Sisters is one of many in the reserve, with others leading to an osage orange tree tunnel and a sycamore ridge. Bring along a sack lunch, as picnic tables and fire rings are provided, and don't forget your binoculars for viewing the abundant birdlife.

POINTS OF INTEREST:

1. *John Bryan State Park*
   This beautiful state park has picnic tables, hiking trails, and camping. Cost for camping is $3.00 per night.

2. *1884 Steel Truss Bridge*
   This is a fairly early metal truss bridge, and was built at the time the wooden covered bridge was becoming obsolete.

3. *Bellbrook Museum and Park*
   Just one block north of the traffic light you'll find the Bellbrook museum, housed in a home built in 1825. Across the street is the small city park where magnetic springs were discovered in 1884. It became an attraction for people seeking the water's healing properties, and a sign above the water fountain still reads "Welcome. Come in and drink freely of the water." The museum is open Saturday and Sunday 2-5. There is no admission charge, but donations are accepted.

4. *Fairview Pioneer Cemetery*
   Stones dating back to 1826 are found here, and include veterans of the War of 1812 and the Civil War.

5. *Sugarcreek Nature Reserve*
   This splendid reserve is open year round for hiking and picnicking. There is no water here, however.

6. *Pioneer Church*
   This M.E. church was originally built in 1807, and rebuilt in 1858.

7. *1910 Railroad Overpass*
   Use caution as you cross this unusual structure, as visibility is obstructed.

8. *Charleton Mill Covered Bridge*
   Located ½ mile from the main route, this beautiful old bridge was built in 1860.

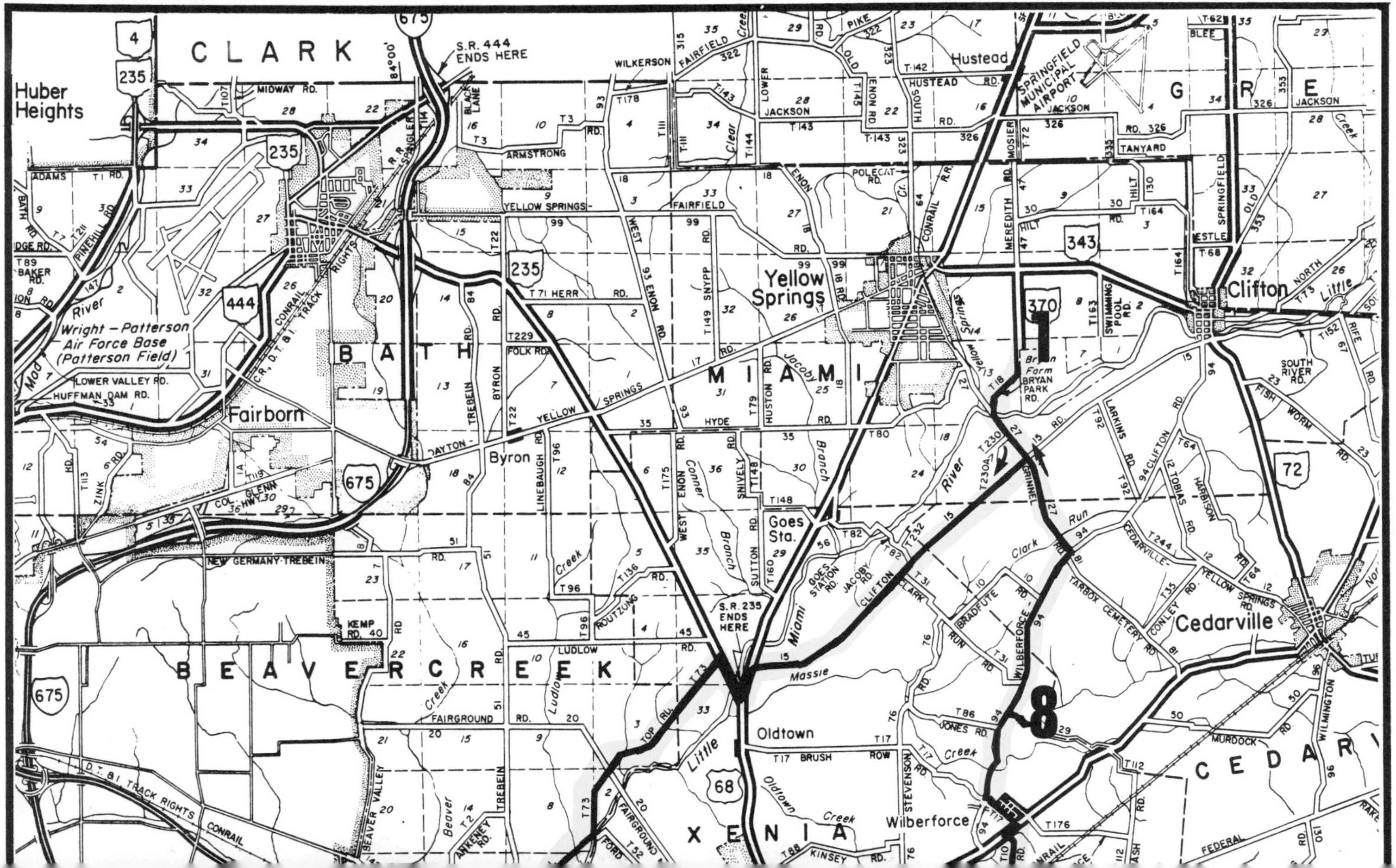
CLARK
S.R. 444 ENDS HERE
Huber Heights
Wright – Patterson Air Force Base (Patterson Field)
Fairborn
BATH
MIAMI
BEAVERCREEK
XENIA
CEDAR
Yellow Springs
Hustead
Springfield Municipal Airport
Clifton
Byron
Goes Sta.
S.R. 235 ENDS HERE
Oldtown
Wilberforce
Cedarville
Bryan Farm
Bryan Park Rd.
Midway Rd.
Armstrong
Yellow Springs - Fairfield
Dayton - Yellow Springs
Lower Valley Rd.
Huffman Dam Rd.
Col. Glenn Hwy.
New Germany-Trebein
Fairground Rd.
Ludlow
Kemp Rd.
Beaver Valley
Conrail
D.T. & I. Track Rights
Linebaugh Rd.
Byron Rd.
Trebein Rd.
West Enon Rd.
Hyde Rd.
Huston Rd.
Sutton Rd.
Snively
Goes Station Rd.
Jacoby Rd.
Clifton Rd.
Clark Run Rd.
Bradfute Rd.
Wilberforce - Clifton Rd.
Tarbox Cemetery Rd.
Grinnel
Larkins Rd.
Tobias Rd.
Harbison
Yellow Springs Rd.
Conley Rd.
Stevenson Rd.
Brush Row
Jones Rd.
Murdock Rd.
Wilmington Rd.
Federal Rd.
Fish Worm Rd.
South River Rd.
Rife Rd.
North
Jackson
Tanyard
Springfield
Hilt Rd.
Meredith Rd.
Mosier Rd.
Enon Rd.
Fairfield
Wilkerson
Black Lane
Spangler
Adams
Pinehill Rd.
Bath Rd.
Zink Rd.
Little Miami River
Massie Creek
Oldtown Creek
Conner Branch
Jacoby Branch
Beaver Creek
Ludlow Creek
Mad River
Yellow Springs Creek
Clear Creek
4
235
444
675
343
370
72
68
1
8

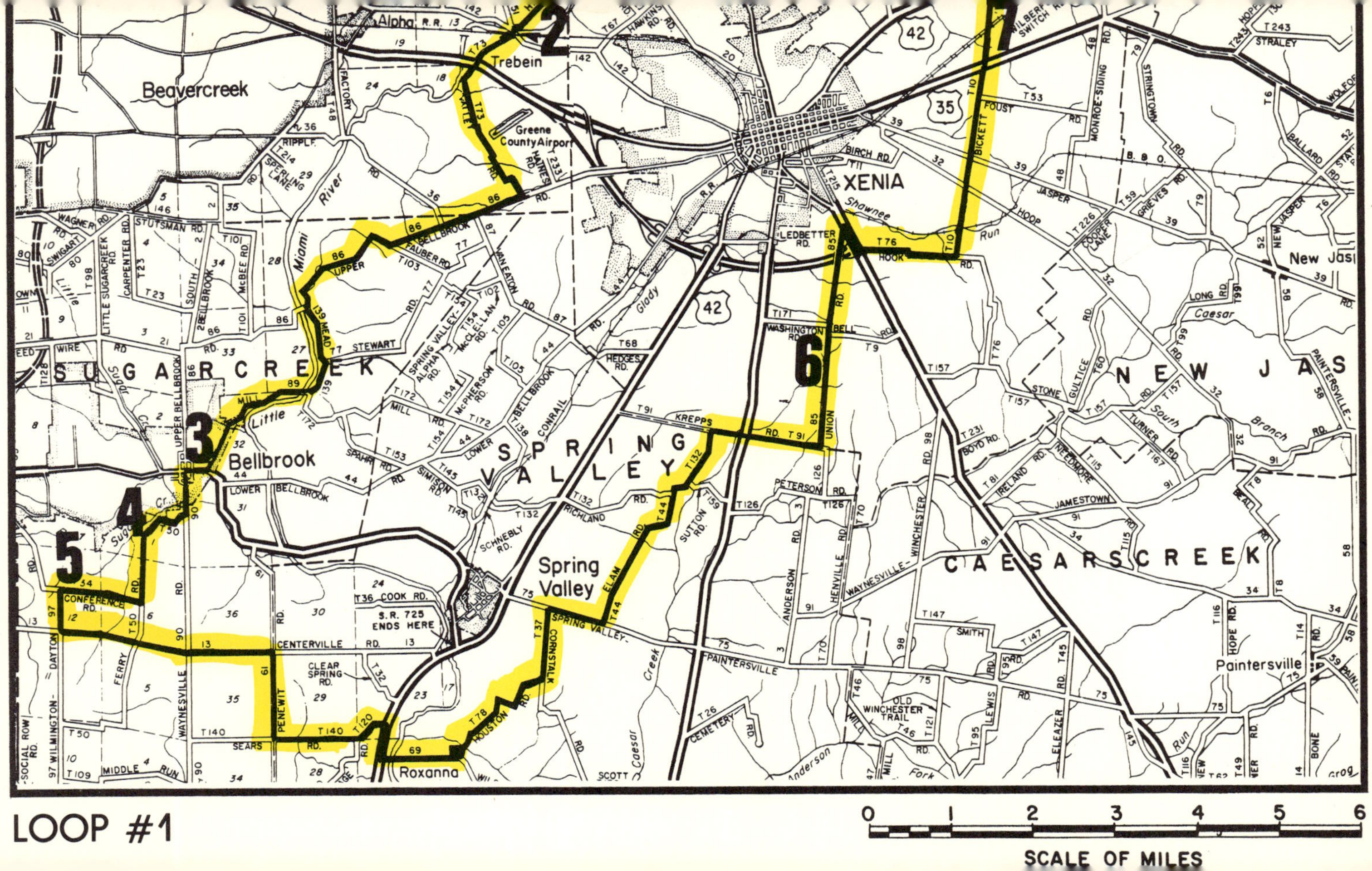
Beavercreek
Trebein
Alpha
Greene County Airport
XENIA
New Jas
Bellbrook
Spring Valley
Roxanna
Paintersville
SUGARCREEK
SPRING VALLEY
CAESARSCREEK
NEW JAS
1
2
3
4
5
6
0 1 2 3 4 5 6
SCALE OF MILES

LOOP #1

LOOP #2

Distance: 27 miles

Terrain: Rather hilly

County: Greene

Tecumseh and Friend

This beautiful loop takes you over rolling countryside, through pastured farmland, and along lovely streams. The ride is rather hilly in places, and rewards the tourer with panoramic views. Covered bridges, old mills, pioneer cemeteries, a nature preserve, and more are found on this trip. It is one of two rides from John Bryan State Park, and when coupled with the Three Sisters loop, provides two days of riding for campers.

This ride leads into the very heart of the old Shawnee nation in Ohio, as well as into the hearts of its greatest leader and his pioneer friend. The Shawnee village of Chalagatha (not to be confused with present day Chilicothe, which was named in honor of the Shawnee village) bustled on the current site of Oldtown, and is the destination of this history-filled ride. Chalagatha was the home of Tecumseh, born in 1768 under a magnificent shooting star. A striking physical figure and born leader, Tecumseh also had the gift of prophecy, and predicted eclipses, earthquakes, and the outcome of great battles. After the defeat of the Indians in 1795, Tecumseh did not participate in the signing of the Greenville Treaty with General Anthony Wayne (see Treaty Line Ride), which pushed the Indians northward. Instead, he began laying the groundwork for uniting all the tribes of North America in a great effort to sweep the settlers back to the eastern sea.

At about this same time, in 1799, James Galloway, a pioneer from Kentucky and Revolutionary War soldier, moved into the valley to establish his home, the first log cabin in the area. As Mr. Galloway and his family were looking over the land, they encountered Tecumseh, and learned that it was Tecumseh's home before the war and treaty pushed him out. Feeling compassion for the displaced warrior, James Galloway told Tecumseh that his door would always be open to him. Thus began one of the few friendships the great Shawnee made with the settlers. So close did Tecumseh and Galloway become that Tecumseh asked for the hand of

Galloway's daughter, Rebecca, in marriage. After considerable agonizing on both sides, it was decided that the union could not work in such troubled times. To protect these people that he loved, however, Tecumseh ordered his warriors not to harm women and children when the war came. In 1812 the war did come, and Tecumseh died in battle, serving his people as a British warrior against the Americans.

On this ride, you will find a memorial to Tecumseh, as well as the pioneer cemetery in which James Galloway and his family are buried.

POINTS OF INTEREST:

1. *John Bryan State Park*
   Hiking trails, picnic tables, and camping are available at the park. Camping costs $3.00 per night.

2. *Grinnell Mill*
   At the bottom of a steep descent is the old Grinnell mill, which is now a private residence.

3. *Grinnell Covered Bridge*
   This bridge, built between 1860 and 1870, formerly stood on Cemetery Road, and was moved to a field just northwest of the old Grinnell mill.

4. *Glen Helen Nature Preserve*
   This nature preserve has beautiful nature trails, the "yellow springs", a swing bridge, and many interesting natural rock formations. The preserve is open during daylight hours, and the trailside museum is open Tues.-Fri. 10-12, Sat. & Sun. 12-5:30, closed Mon. To reach the preserve, turn right on Grinnell for 1¼ miles, then right on Corry to the entrance.

5. *Stevenson Road Covered Bridge*
   This historic covered bridge, built in 1873, spans Massie Creek.

6. *Oldtown*
   This is the site of the old Shawnee village of Chalagatha. Several stone markers commemorating Tecumseh, Daniel Boone, and Simon Kenton are found here. The markers are located on U.S. 68 about 100 yards south of Brush Row Road.

7. *Stevenson Cemetery*
   In 1804 the Massie Creek Church Lot and Cemetery was established, and is now known as Stevenson Cemetery. This is the pioneer graveyard where James Galloway and his family are buried, as are many other soldiers of the Revolution. Mr. Galloway's marker indicates that he was "an honest man and pious Christian".

8. *Charleton Mill Covered Bridge*
   This covered bridge was built in 1860, and is located ½ mile east on Charleton Mill Road. This is a nice rest stop where you can watch the stream flow gently under the old bridge.

9. *Clifton Mill*
   In the village of Clifton stands the Clifton Mill, overlooking the Little Miami River at the head of Clifton Gorge. The mill was established in 1803, the year of Ohio statehood. It was destroyed by fire in the 1840's, and rebuilt in 1869. The mill is water powered by the swift Little Miami River. There are many stone ground products for sale, and an enjoyable little restaurant is also located in the mill. Hours: M-F, 8-7, breakfast til 11; Sat. & Sun. 8-8, breakfast til 1. Self-guided tours of the mill are 75¢.

10. *Clifton Gorge*
    This nature preserve has hiking trails and lookout points over the gorge. By following the trail a very short distance, you will come to the "Narrows", where Cornelius Darnell, a member of Daniel Boone's party being held captive at Chalagatha, made a daring escape by leaping 22 feet across the gorge to evade his pursuers and flee to Kentucky. The preserve is a National Natural Landmark.

11. *Young's Dairy (Side Trip)*
    This dairy is open 24 hours a day, and has a bakery on the premises. It is one of the few places in Ohio that can sell raw milk, and their ice cream and milk shakes are excellent. You can even pet the cows at this *real* dairy which is located on the east side of U.S. 68.

12. *Ye Olde Trail Tavern (Side Trip)*
    The tavern is located in Yellow Springs. The village can be reached by taking Route 370 north from John Bryan State Park, then west on Route 343 to U.S. 68, then south into Yellow Springs, a total distance of about 3 miles. The tavern, built in 1827, was the first home in Yellow Springs, then known as Forest Village. The street was originally an Indian trail, and later became part of the stage coach route from Cincinnati to Columbus.

NOTES

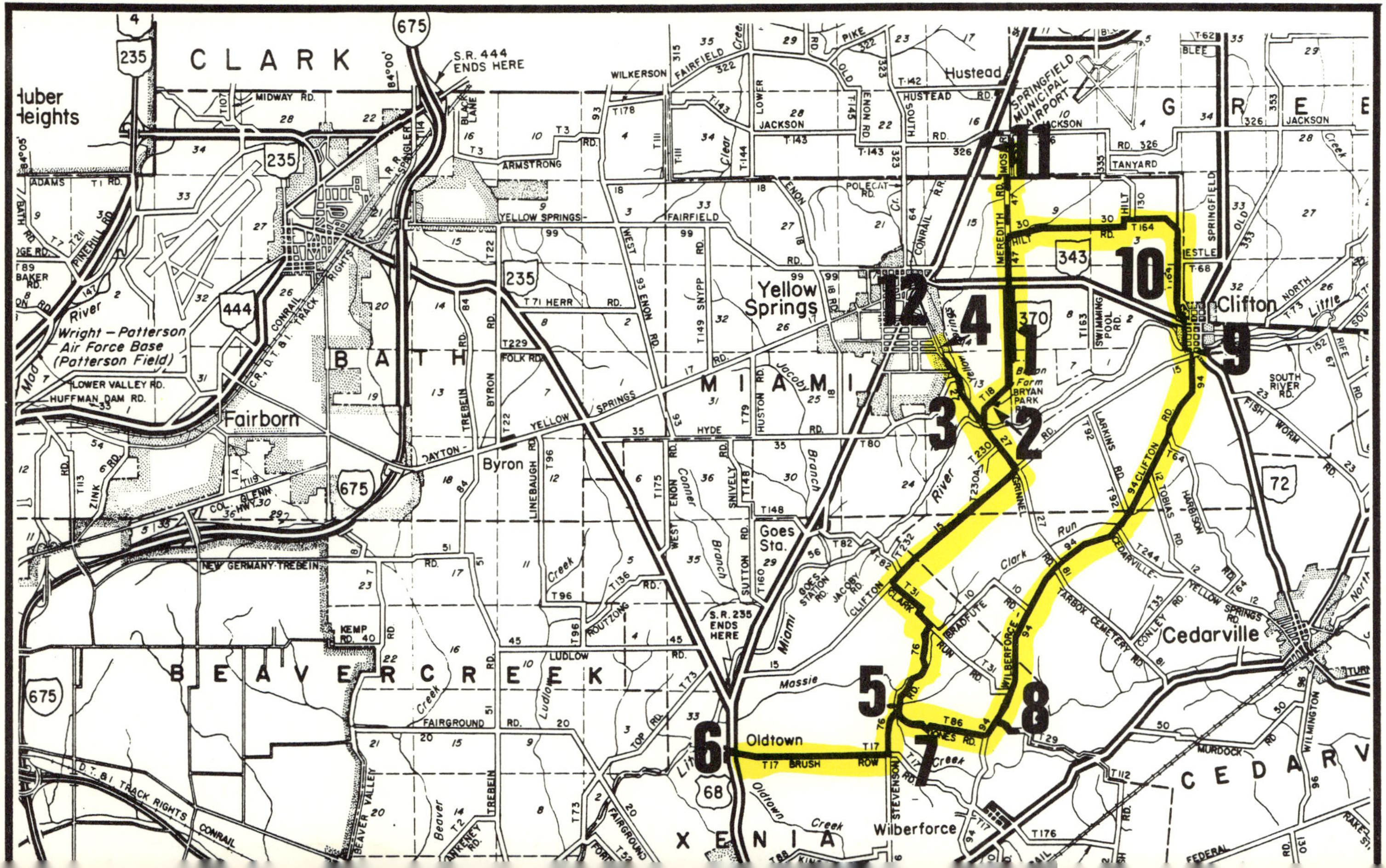

CLARK
GREENE
BATH
MIAMI
BEAVERCREEK
XENIA
CEDARVILLE
Huber Heights
Fairborn
Wright-Patterson Air Force Base (Patterson Field)
Byron
Yellow Springs
Goes Sta.
Clifton
Cedarville
Oldtown
Wilberforce
Hustead
SPRINGFIELD MUNICIPAL AIRPORT
S.R. 444 ENDS HERE
S.R. 235 ENDS HERE
Bryan Farm
BRYAN PARK
1
2
3
4
5
6
7
8
9
10
11
12

LOOP #2

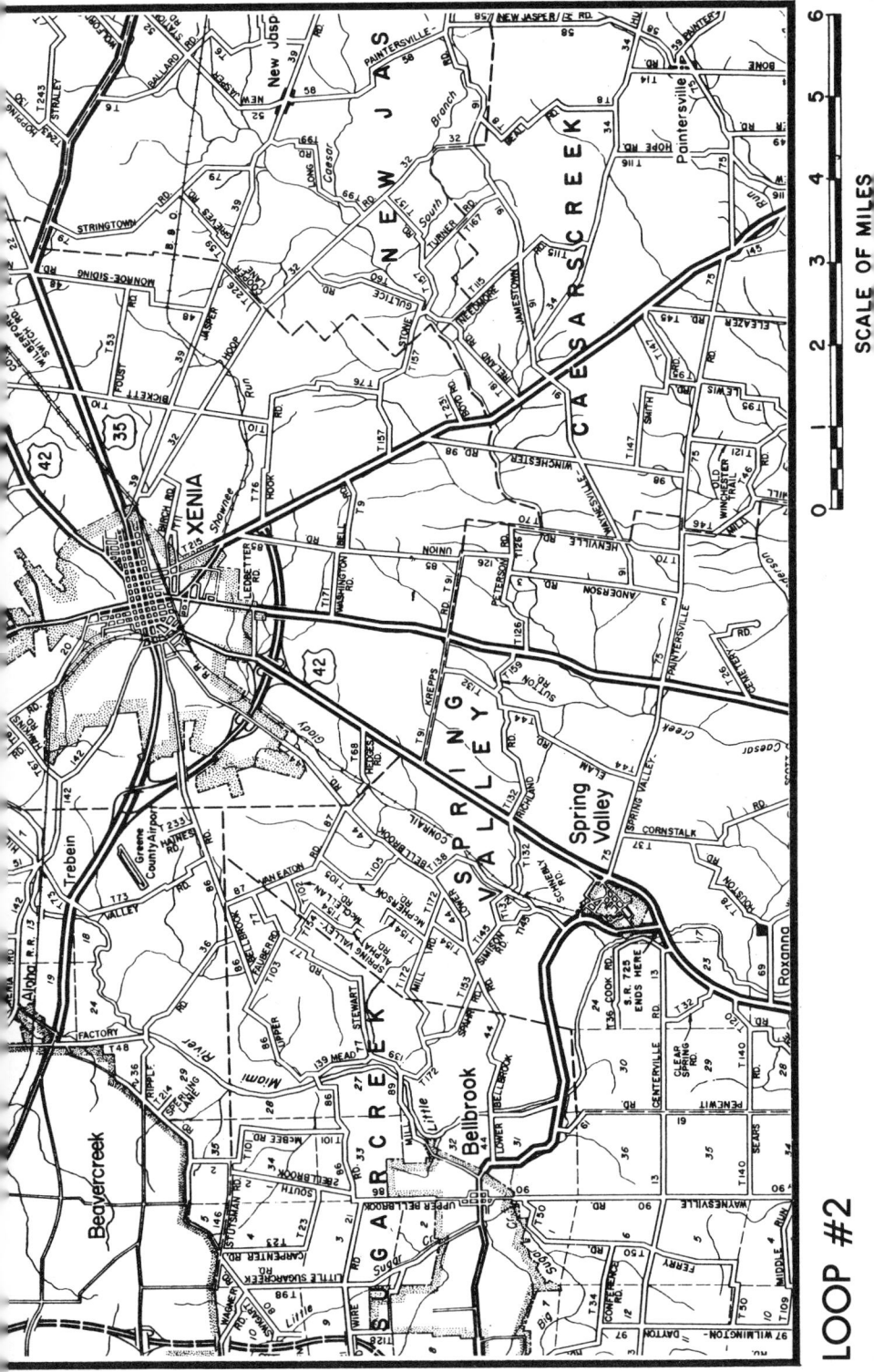

LOOP #3

Distance: 39 miles

Terrain: Flat to gently rolling

County: Champaign

Ice Age Deja Vu

As is typical of the landscape in the till plains of western Central Ohio, this ride takes you over flat to gently rolling countryside, along back roads through broad valleys and open farmland. You may wish to couple this ride with the Mackachack Ride and a campout, as both trips leave from Kiser Lake State Park.

Ohio has played host to a number of guests who came from the north during the Ice Age thousands of years ago, and stayed on after the glacier retreated. This makes it possible for us today to visit these guests, the plants and trees of the north, right in our own backyard. Of course, these trees and plants typical of the northern forests require very special conditions that are not readily found this far south in North America. Fortunately, a cold spring flowing through glacial outwash provides the necessary environment for these northern Michigan and Canadian plants at Cedar Bog. In addition to the northern plants, many prairie plants can also be found here. An unusual stand of arbor vitae, or white cedar, is present in the bog, and another stand this large won't be found without traveling far to the north.

The bog has a characteristic accumulation of peat formed by non-decaying plant material in the oxygen-starved water, and certain places in the bog may quake from this mass of peat being supported on shallow, high volume springs. Therefore, a floating boardwalk is provided to lead you through the bog. Take along your wildflower book to identify the many species found here, or just enjoy a stroll. A checklist of some of the plants you may find here is provided on the next page. If you are visiting during mosquito season, remember to bring your repellent.

POINTS OF INTEREST:

1. *Kiser Lake State Park*
   The park has a swimming beach, picnic tables, hiking trails, and camping.

2. *Nettle Creek Pioneer Cemetery*
   This cemetery has stones dating back to 1818, and veterans of the Revolutionary and Civil Wars are buried here. Several unusual markers fashioned as tree trunks can be found here.

3. *Cedar Bog Nature Preserve*
   Operated and maintained by the Ohio Historical Society, the bog is open for public tours April to September, Saturdays and Sundays at 1:00 and 3:00 P.M. Adults $1.50, children $1.00.

4. *Prince Pioneer Cemetery*
   This small hilltop cemetery has stones dating back to 1834.

Cedar Bog Plant Checklist

MARL MEADOW:
- [ ] Calopogon Orchid
- [ ] False Asphodel
- [ ] Bunchflower
- [ ] Marsh Violet
- [ ] Kalm's Lobelia
- [ ] Grass-of-Parnassus
- [ ] Tuberous Indian Plantain
- [ ] Chara
- [ ] Cotton Grass
- [ ] Round-Leaf Sundew
- [ ] Ohio Goldenrod
- [ ] Riddell's Goldenrod
- [ ] Purple Gerardia
- [ ] Ladies-Tresses Orchid
- [ ] Fringed Gentian

FEN MEADOW:
- [ ] Shrubby Cinquefoil
- [ ] Alder Buckthorn
- [ ] Swamp Birch
- [ ] Ninebark
- [ ] Poison Sumac
- [ ] Alder
- [ ] Nannyberry

FEN MEADOW WILDFLOWERS:
- [ ] Canada Mayflower
- [ ] Starflower
- [ ] Pink Lady's Slipper
- [ ] Yellow Lady's Slipper
- [ ] New England Aster

SHRUB MEADOW ZONE:
- [ ] Arbor Vitae (White Cedar)
- [ ] Tamarack

PRAIRIE SPECIES:
- [ ] Indian Grass
- [ ] Prairie Cordgrass
- [ ] Big Bluestem
- [ ] Queen-of-the-Prairie
- [ ] Nodding Wild Onion
- [ ] Prairie Dock
- [ ] Spiked Blazing Star
- [ ] Sneezeweed

NOTES

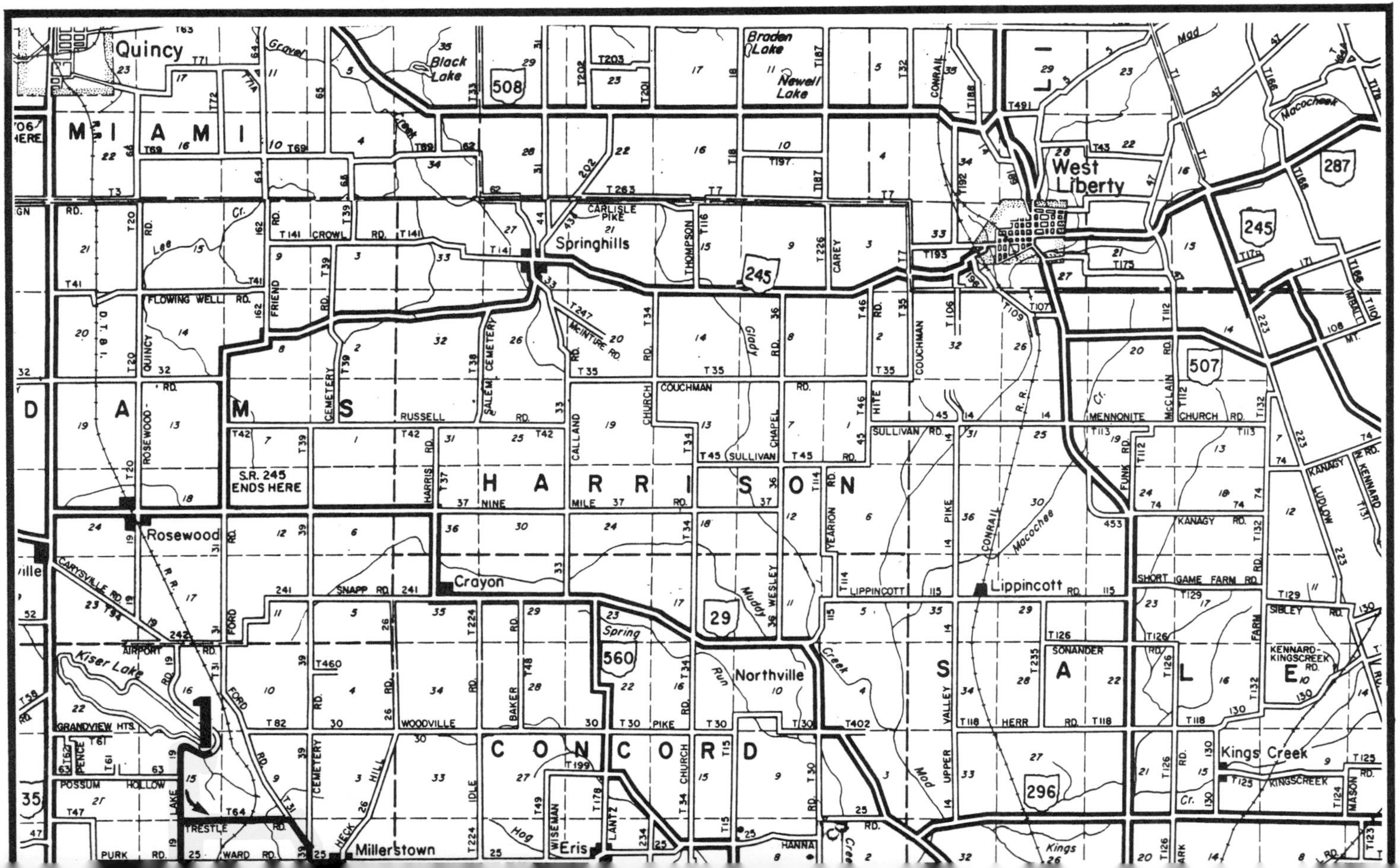
Quincy
MIAMI
ADAMS
HARRISON
SALEM
CONCORD
West Liberty
Springhills
Rosewood
Crayon
Lippincott
Northville
Kings Creek
Millerstown
Eris
Black Lake
Braden Lake
Newell Lake
Kiser Lake
S.R. 245 ENDS HERE
CARLISLE PIKE
FLOWING WELL RD.
ROSEWOOD - QUINCY RD.
COUCHMAN RD.
CHURCH RD.
SULLIVAN RD.
MENNONITE CHURCH RD.
McCLAIN RD.
NINE MILE RD.
SNAPP RD.
LIPPINCOTT RD.
SHORT GAME FARM RD.
KANAGY RD.
KENNARD-KINGSCREEK RD.
KINGSCREEK
CARYSVILLE RD.
AIRPORT RD.
GRANDVIEW HTS.
POSSUM HOLLOW
WOODVILLE
HECK HILL
CEMETERY
SALEM CEMETERY
RUSSELL RD.
CALLAND
THOMPSON
CAREY
YEARION
WESLEY
PIKE
VALLEY
UPPER VALLEY PIKE
HERR RD.
SONANDER
SIBLEY RD.
LUDLOW
N. KENNARD
CONRAIL
Macochee
Mad
Muddy
Spring Run
Glady
Hog
Mad Creek
Kings
508
245
287
507
29
560
296
453

LOOP #3

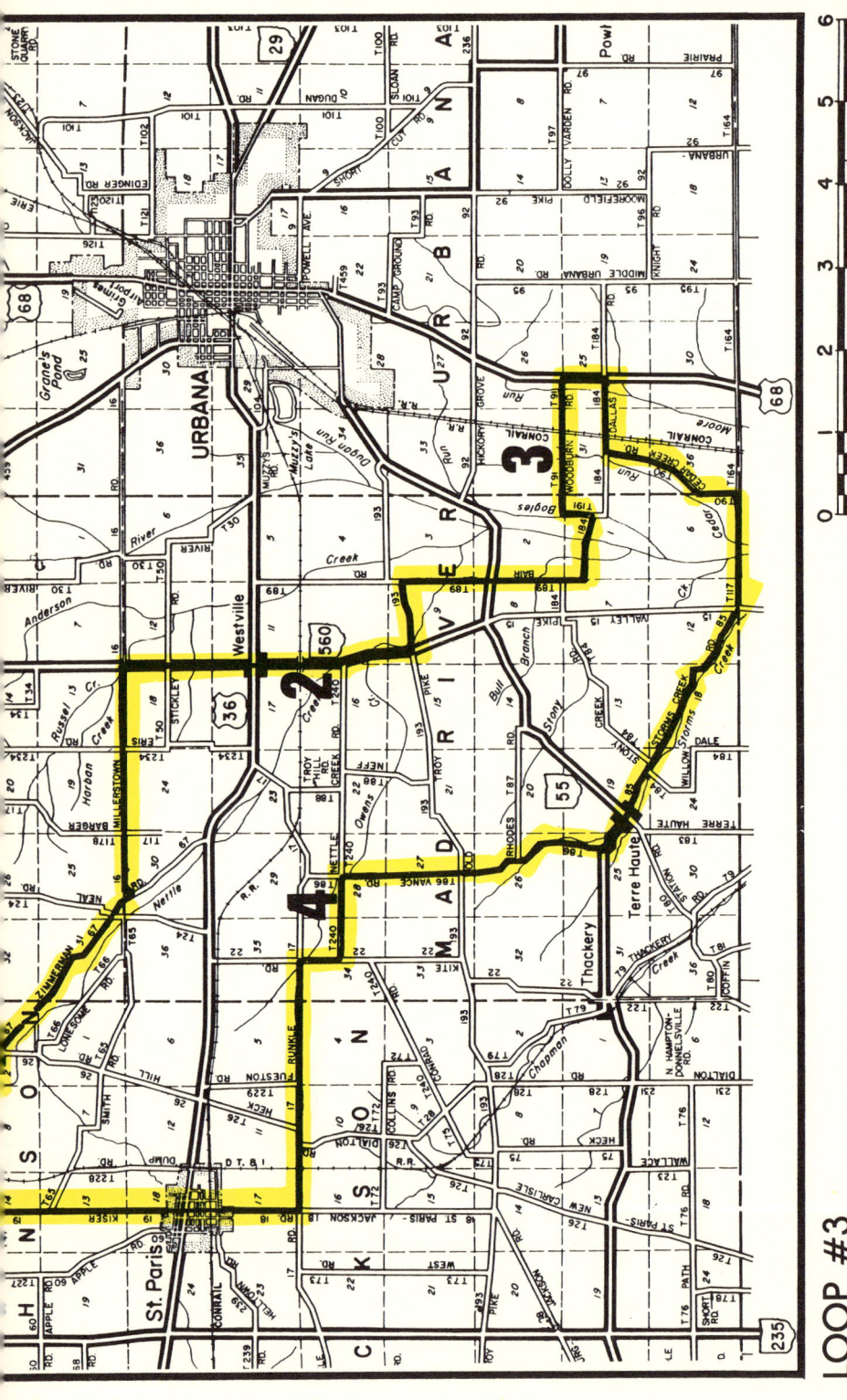

LOOP #4

Distance: 39 miles

Terrain: Flat to gently rolling

County: Champaign/Logan

The Mackachack Ride

Diversity is the hallmark of this 39 mile ride, one of two to begin at Kiser Lake State Park, where camping is available. Castles and caverns, log cabins, pioneer cemeteries, and cascading creeks are all part of this loop through historic Champaign county. In the fall, migrating Canada geese can be seen on the ponds that dot the gently rolling countryside as you travel these quiet back lanes. But were you to travel back in time exactly two centuries ago, you would have been in a time of turmoil and conflict on this very ground known to the Indians as Mackachack, or "Smiling Valley".

All that is left of Mackachack Town now is a small roadside marker that hints at the events of the 1780's. At this site, in October of 1786, an officer of General Benjamin Logan's army, Major Simon Kenton, watched from cover as a deserter from the troops warned the Indians of an impending attack from the army; he also saw the Shawnees kill the deserter on the spot after giving them the warning, for they had no respect for one who would betray his own people. Kenton returned to General Logan with word of the betrayal, and it was decided that they would join forces with Colonel Daniel Boone and attack the villages as soon as possible. When the attack came the next morning, only a few warriors were in the village, and it wasn't much of a skirmish. Chief Moluntha, aged King of the Shawnees, was captured, and after being promised protection by General Logan, was slain by a deranged army captain, who was in turn assaulted by his own troops and later court-martialed. The army went on to destroy eight Indian towns located in the Mackachack area.

This wasn't the first time that strife, or Simon Kenton, had come to Mackachack. Eight years previous, in 1778, Kenton had been captured by the Shawnees, far to the south of Mackachack. Due to his great fame among the Indians as the greatest fighter and frontiersman alive, he was sentenced to die in a most grueling and public way. He was marched from Indian town to Indian town, from Chalagatha to Mackachack, nine towns in all, and forced to run a gauntlet each time. Miraculously, he was able to escape death time after time, until he was "rescued" by British soldiers who wanted to interrogate him at Detroit. The Shawnees came to believe that Simon Kenton must have been under the protection of the Great Spirit and therefore was not to be harmed. And, indeed, Simon Kenton eventually died in his bed in nearby Urbana at the age of eighty-eight.

Mackachack Town is gone, but the Smiling Valley remains with a large number of interesting historical and natural sites that provide a full day of exploring for the modern adventurer.

POINTS OF INTEREST:

1. *Kiser Lake State Park*
   The park has a swimming beach, picnic tables, hiking trails, and camping.

2. *Mackachack Town Historical Marker*

3. *Castle Piatt Mac-A-Cheek*
   Built by General Abram Sanders Piatt in 1864 in the Norman-French chateau style, the castle contains furnishings up to 250 years old. The castle is open daily Spring to Fall.

   Piatt Log Home
   This newly restored log home located just south of the castle was originally built in 1828 by federal Judge Benjamin Piatt. When the judge was away from home, the cabin served as a station on the underground railroad under the auspices of Piatt's wife, Elizabeth, an ardent abolitionist. The home is now open to the public, and houses a gift and antique shop. Open Monday-Saturday 11-5, Sunday 1-5.

   Piatt Cemetery
   Located a short distance south of the log home on a hilltop, this old overgrown cemetery has stones dating back to 1808.

4. *Ohio Caverns*
   These are the largest and perhaps most colorful caverns in the state, and boast the Crystal King, the largest crystal white stalactite in Ohio. Open year round, admission $5.00 for adults, and includes a guided tour.

5. *Century Old Meeting House*
    Built in 1881, the Mt. Tabor Church Building is the site of a reading of a historic narrative on summer Sundays beginning at 2:00 P.M. The old cemetery on the south side of the church has stones dating back to 1817, and gravestones of veterans of the Revolutionary War, War of 1812, and the Civil War are found here.

NOTES

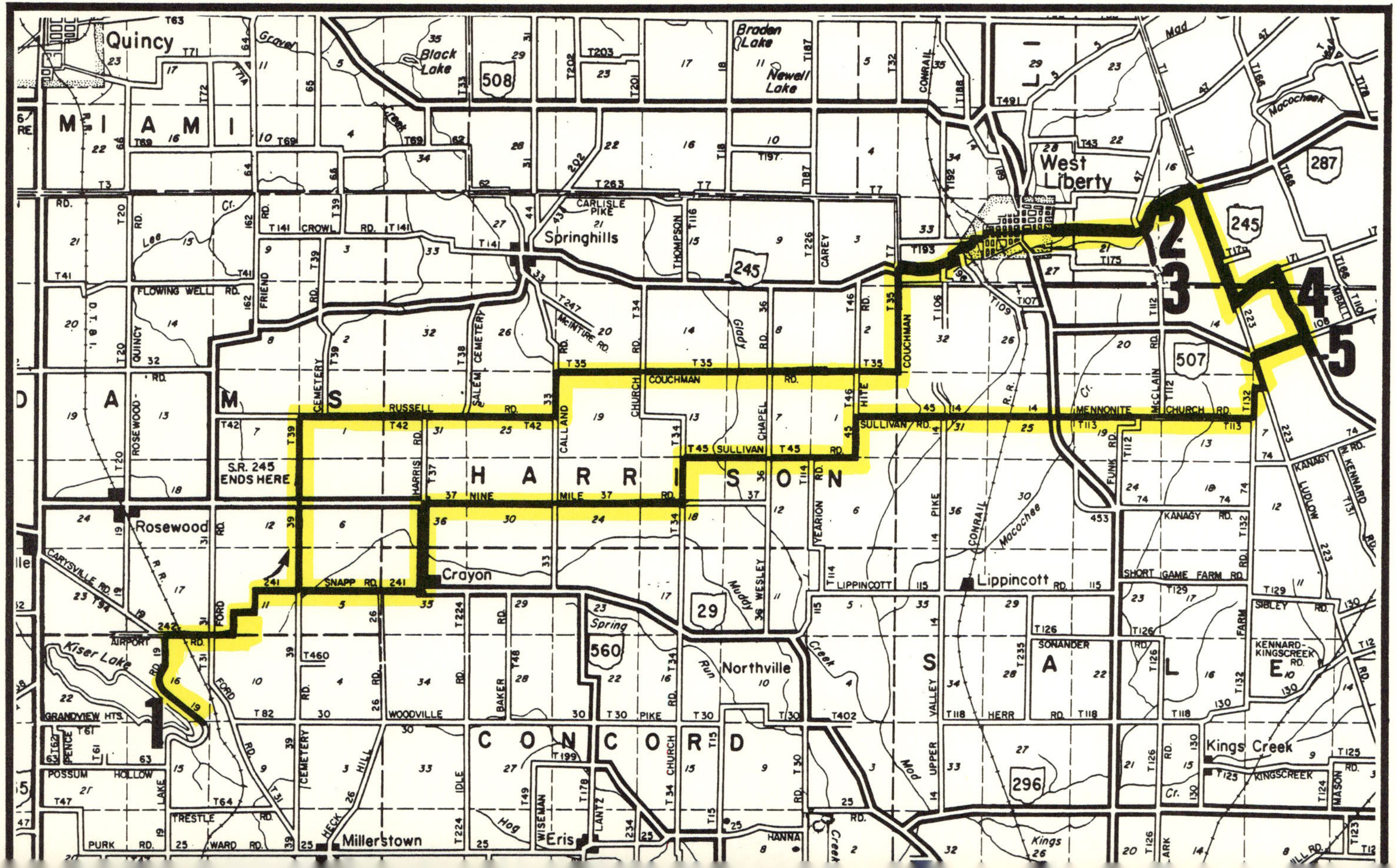

Quincy
West Liberty
Springhills
Rosewood
Crayon
Lippincott
Northville
Millerstown
Eris
Kings Creek
Kiser Lake
Black Lake
Broden Lake
Newell Lake
MIAMI
HARRISON
CONCORD
SALEM
ADAMS
S.R. 245 ENDS HERE
COUCHMAN RD.
SULLIVAN RD.
NINE MILE RD.
SNAPP RD.
MENNONITE CHURCH RD.
RUSSELL RD.
1
2
3
4
5

LOOP #4

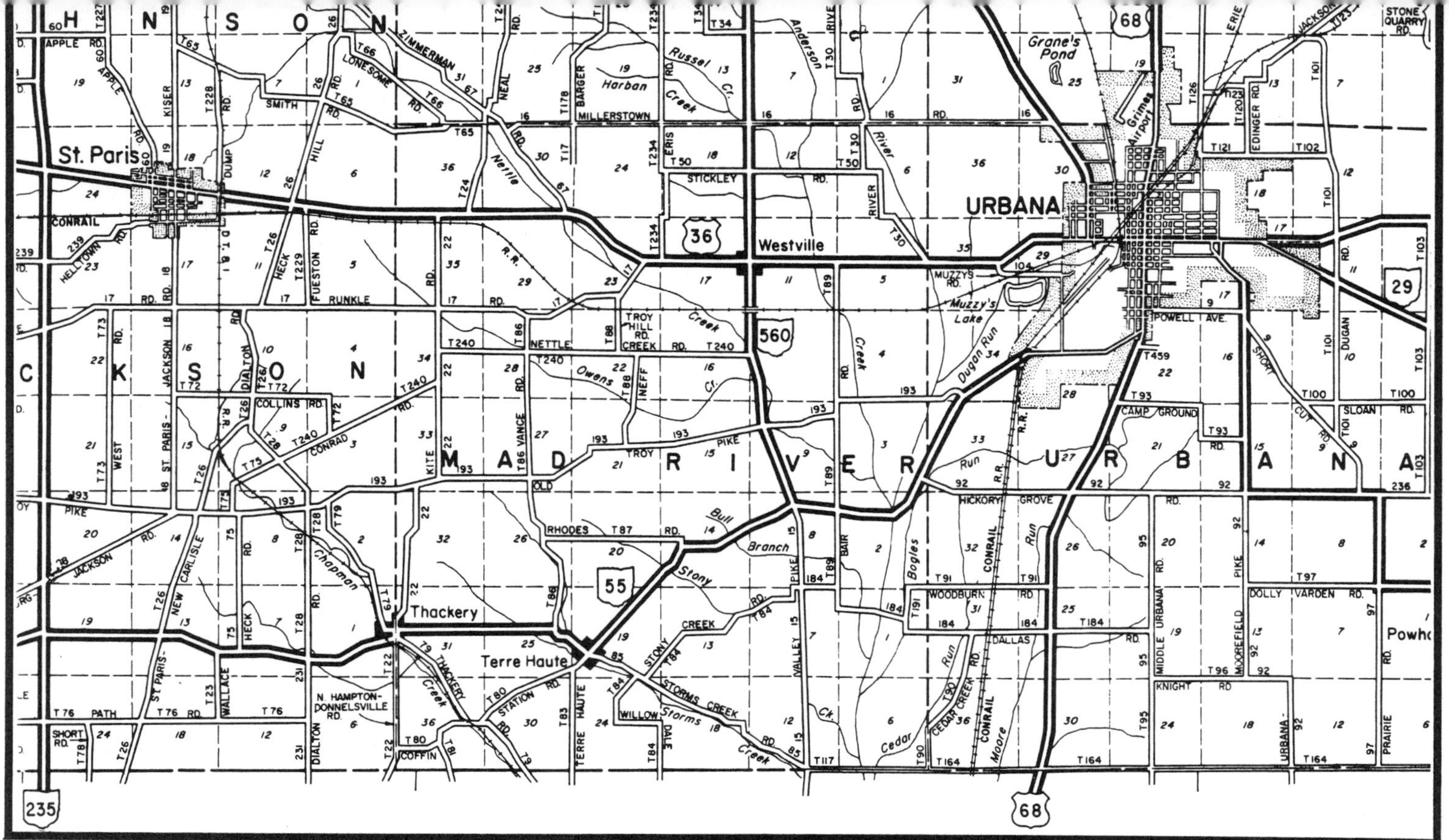

0 1 2 3 4 5 6

SCALE OF MILES

LOOP #5

Distance: 45 miles

Terrain: Flat

County: Madison

Prairie Flower Ride

Rich, flat farmland is the setting of this Madison County ride. The area is fertile, and you will see large farms along the way. But as you ride to Smith Cemetery Prairie, cast your imagination back about 175 years, and visualize an area vastly different from what you see today. Put yourself into the shoes of Charles and Alvira Andrews, one of the first families to settle here in "The Barrens", as these Darby Plains were then called.

Moving into this area in 1814, the Andrews' were not settling rich farmland, but rather moving into an almost worthless extensive wet prairie, quite similar to the tall grass prairies of the west. The dense prairie grass grew to a height of eight feet, and the poorly drained land was covered with water most of the year. But as is characteristic of prairies, the land became dry in the fall and subject to raging prairie fires, a device that protects the succession of prairie plants but endangers people and slows settlement. The whole area was described as a sea of prairie grasses and colorful prairie wildflowers.

A few years after the arrival of the Andrews', their five-year old daughter, Almira, became ill and died, and was the first person laid to rest in what is now called Smith Cemetery. Other family members joined her as the years went by, until in 1834 the land was transferred to the Darby Township trustees, and the original owners left the plains for good.

The original vast prairie has all but disappeared, except for some scatterings of burr oak trees and a few patches of prairie plants. Appropriately enough, the best remnant of the prairie is found at Smith Cemetery, where the settlers now rest in the same prairie soil they settled. This sod still supports relicts of the original prairie plant life with its beautiful prairie wildflowers. The Ohio Department of Natural Resources manages this plot to perpetuate the prairie flora and preserve the historic tombstones, which are hidden in the prairie grasses.

Thirty species of native prairie plants have been identified in Smith Cemetery, and a checklist of some of these is provided here. Take along your wildflower book and a sack lunch for this ride, and see how many of these beautiful prairie plants you can identify. The peak blooming time for these wildflowers is late July through most of August.

You'll return to Madison Lake on quiet country lanes and cross over a charming old steel bridge. A swim at the park awaits you after a hot day in the prairie.

POINTS OF INTEREST:

1. *Madison Lake State Park*
   This state park has a small swimming beach and picnic area. There is no camping here.

2. *Red Brick Tavern*
   Built in 1837, William Henry Harrison and Henry Clay were guests here. Located in Lafayette, it continues to operate as a restaurant and tavern.

3. *May Flag Farm Log Cabin*
   The gateposts of this private log cabin residence indicate the farm was established in 1818, making it one of the earliest settlements in the area. The cabin is typical of the dwellings of that time.

4. *Smith Cemetery Prairie Nature Preserve*
   It's easy to ride past this small preserve, as it is not marked on the road. Exactly one-half mile after turning onto this road is an opening into a farm field. The cemetery lies about seventy-five yards back into the field.

5. *1897 Steel Truss Bridge over Little Darby Creek*

6. *Lower Glade Pioneer Cemetery*
   Several examples of early tombstone art and materials can be seen here.

Prairie Plant Checklist

- [ ] Wild Garlic
- [ ] Big Bluestem
- [ ] Little Bluestem
- [ ] Canadian Anemone
- [ ] Smooth Aster
- [ ] New Jersey Tea
- [ ] Gray Dogwood
- [ ] Purple Coneflower
- [ ] Gray Willow
- [ ] Whorled Rosinweed
- [ ] Stiff Goldenrod
- [ ] Indian Grass

- [ ] Flowering Spurge
- [ ] Biennial Guara
- [ ] Ox-Eye
- [ ] Prairie False Indigo
- [ ] Wild Bergamot
- [ ] Virginia Mountain Mint
- [ ] Gray-Headed Coneflower
- [ ] Black-Eyed Susan
- [ ] Prairie Cord Grass
- [ ] Skunk Meadow-Rue
- [ ] Golden Alexanders

NOTES

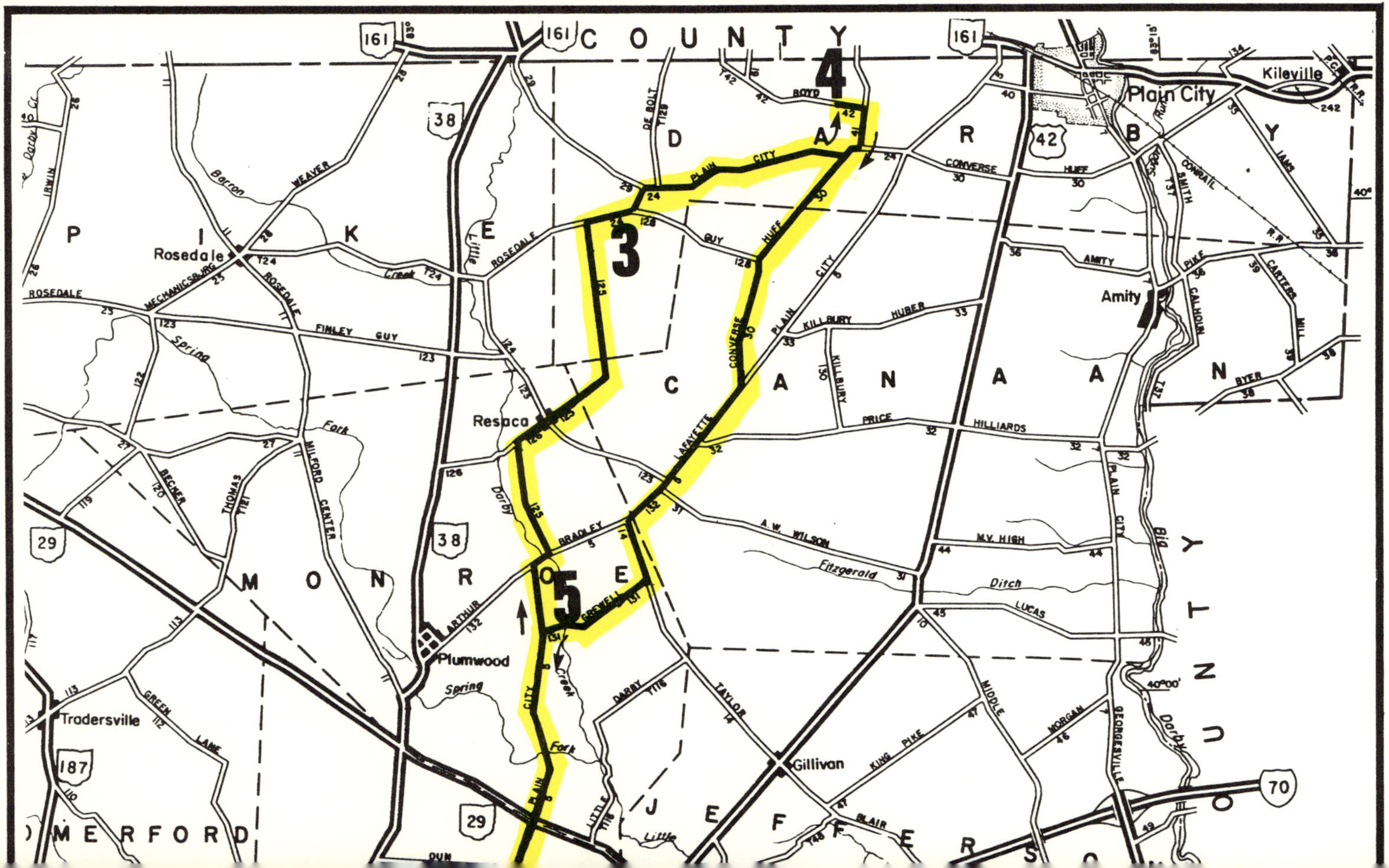
COUNTY
DARBY
CANAAN
PIKE
MONROE
JEFFERSON
UNION COUNTY
Plain City
Kileville
Amity
Rosedale
Resaca
Plumwood
Tradersville
Gillivan
3
4
5
PLAIN CITY
CONVERSE
HUFF
LAFAYETTE
GUY
BRADLEY
BOYD
DE BOLT
ROSEDALE
MECHANICSBURG
WEAVER
IRWIN
FINLEY GUY
MILFORD CENTER
THOMAS
BECHER
GREEN LANE
ARTHUR
KILLBURY
HUBER
PRICE
HILLIARDS
A.W. WILSON
M.V. HIGH
LUCAS
MIDDLE
MORGAN
GEORGESVILLE
KING PIKE
BLAIR
TAYLOR
DARBY
SMITH
IAMS
CONRAIL
AMITY
PIKE
CALHOUN
CARTERS MILL
BYER
Barron
Spring
Fork
Darby
Little
Creek
Fitzgerald
Ditch
Big
40°00'
83°15'
161
38
42
29
187
70

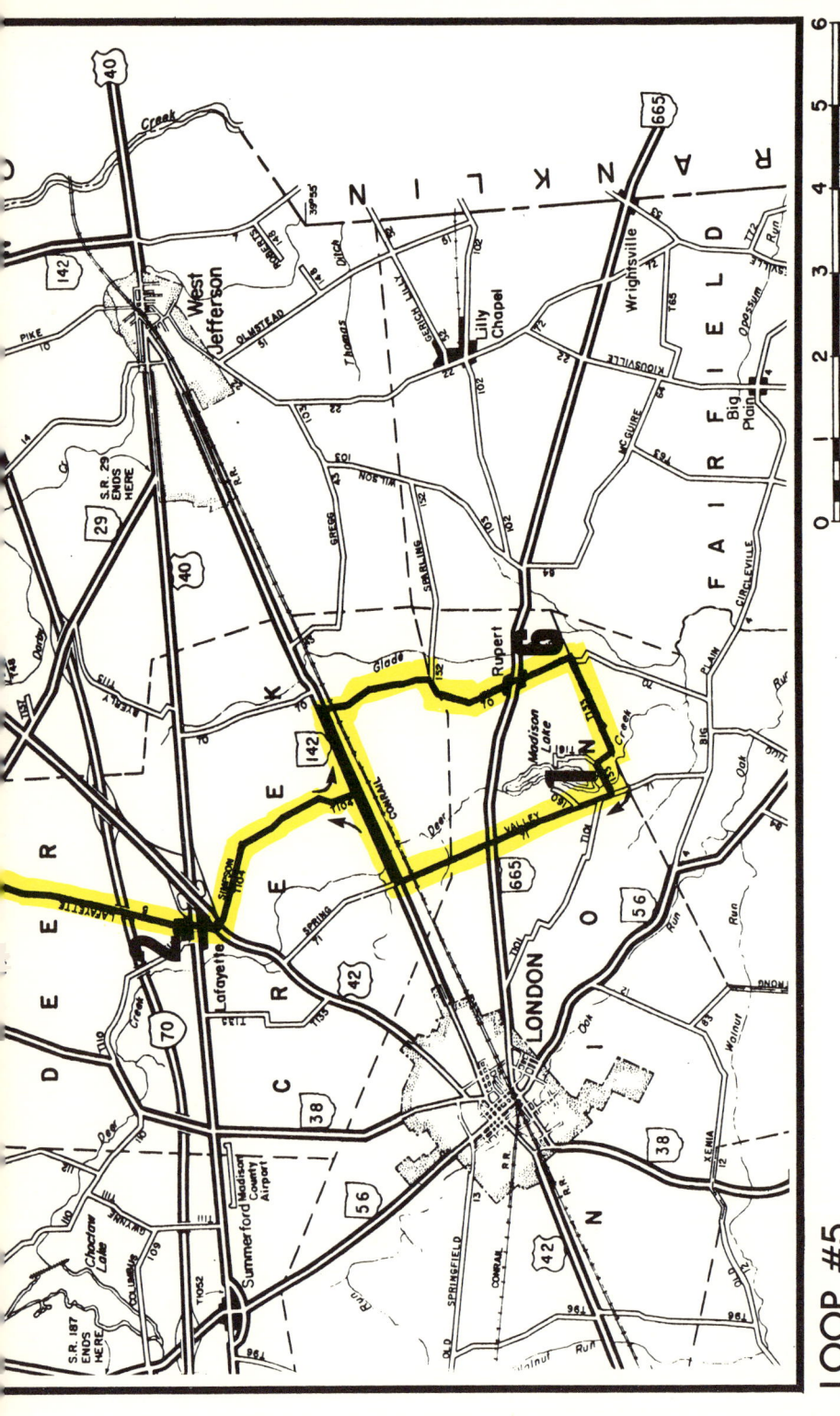

LOOP #5

LOOP #6

Distance: 44 miles

Terrain: Flat

County: Madison/Pickaway

Stage Coach Ride

    This 44 mile route takes the rider from Madison Lake State Park through mostly open level farmland and over a few small hills along Darby Creek near Orient. You'll pass by a cemetery dating back to the early nineteenth century, and cross over two metal truss bridges built around the turn of the twentieth century. These back country roads provide for a most enjoyable bike ride, but the destination of this trip, Green's Heritage Museum, takes you back to the "not-so-good old days" of stage coach travel, when most passengers would have been more than happy to trade their coach seat for your bike seat!

    The stage coach traveler of the nineteenth century had more than potholes with which to contend. Charles Dickens, visiting America in 1842, traveled by stage coach from Cincinnati to Tiffin, and stopped overnight at the newly constructed Neil House in Columbus. He was pleased to see that the road from Cincinnati to Columbus had been of macadam, a rare blessing allowing for speeds of up to 6 miles per hour. Assuming a continuation of such good fortune, Dickens had packed away cheeses and drink to enjoy on the road to Tiffin, a journey he described in *American Notes:* "At one time we were all flung together in a heap at the bottom of the coach, and at another we were crushing our heads against the roof. Now one side was down deep in the mire, and we were holding on to the other. Now the coach was rearing up in the air in a frantic state with all four horses standing at the top of an insurmountable eminence, looking cooly back at us as if to say 'Unharness us. It can't be done.' A great portion of the way was over what is called a corduroy road, which is made by throwing trunks of trees into a marsh, and leaving them to settle there. The very slightest of the jolts with which the ponderous carriage fell from log to log was enough, it seemed, to have dislocated all the bones in the human body. Not once that day did the coach make the smallest approach to one's experience of the proceedings of any sort of vehicle that goes on wheels."

The ride mapped out on this journey passes over paved country roads that would have made Dickens' mouth water. The route leads to Green's Heritage Museum, where no less than 35 different stage coaches, surreys, and sleighs can be seen under one roof. Beautifully restored, they provide an excellent look at yesteryear's travel. An 1800's general store, log cabin, and blacksmith shop can also be found at the museum. The return portion of the ride pleasantly completes this loop, with a swim at Madison Lake adding a welcome finishing touch.

POINTS OF INTEREST:

1. *Madison Lake State Park*
   The park is open daily, and has picnic tables and a swimming beach. There is no camping.

2. *Lower Glade Pioneer Cemetery*
   Early pioneers and Civil War veterans are buried in this old graveyard.

3. *1885 Steel Truss Bridge*
   This large beautiful bridge was erected over Darby Creek in 1885, at the time covered bridge construction was waning. The late 1800's were a time of overlap for the two types of bridges.

4. *Green's Heritage Museum*
   Open 9 to dark in the summer, and by appointment in the winter. Admission is $2.50 for adults, $1.00 for children.

5. *1918 Steel Truss Bridge*

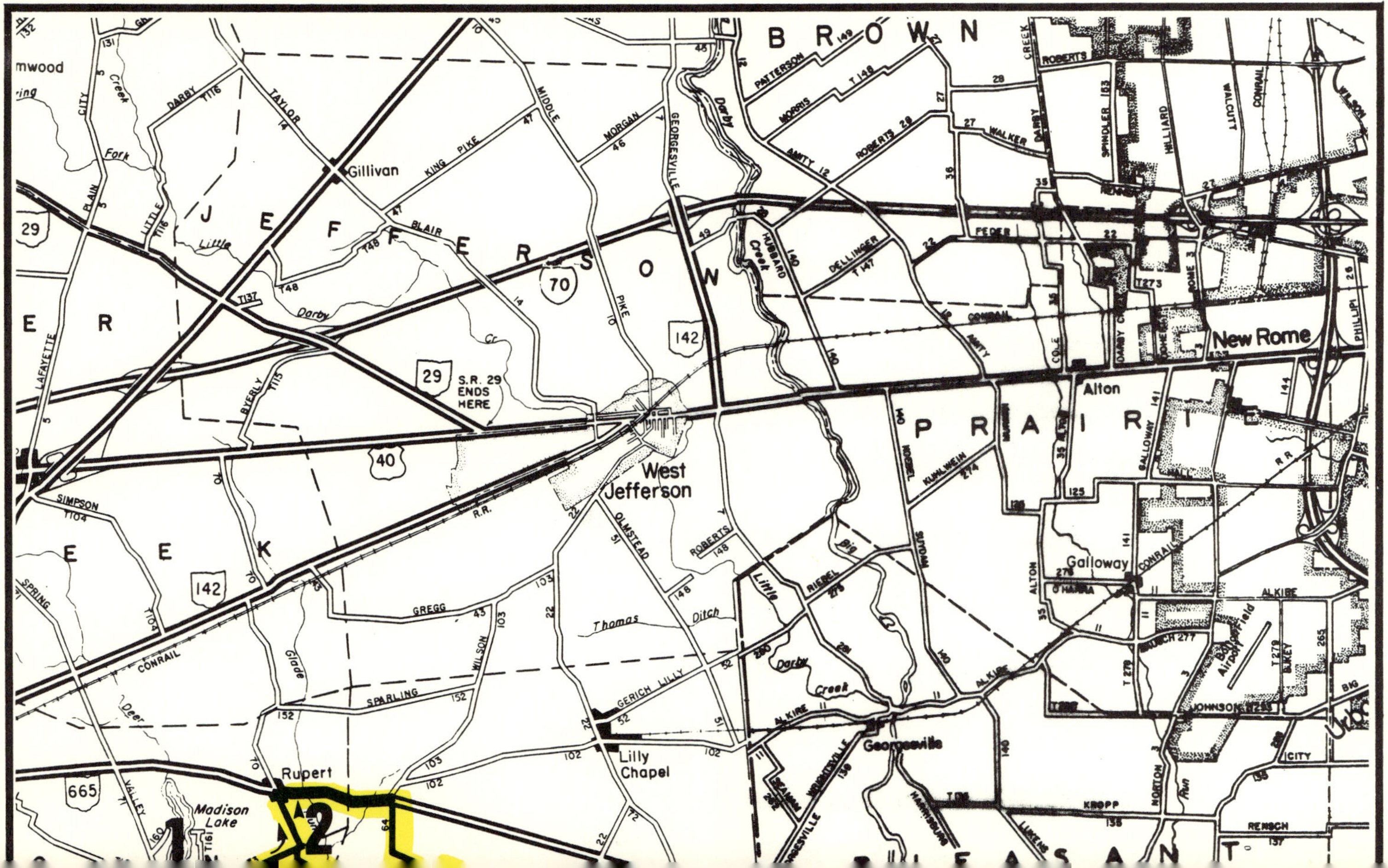
BROWN
JEFFERSON
PRAIRIE
PLEASANT
West Jefferson
New Rome
Alton
Galloway
Georgesville
Lilly Chapel
Rupert
Gillivan
Madison Lake
S.R. 29 ENDS HERE
Darby Creek
Little Darby Creek
Big Darby Creek
Hubbard Creek
Thomas Ditch
Glade
Bolton Airport Field
Roberts
Spindler
Hilliard
Walcutt
Conrail
Georgesville
Middle
Morgan
King Pike
Blair
Taylor
Pike
Gregg
Wilson
Sparling
Olmstead
Gerich Lilly
Alkire
Suydam
Norton
Kropp
Rensch
Johnson
Harrisburg
Lukens
Lafayette
Simpson
Spring
Valley
Plain City
Byerly
Amity
Patterson
Morris
Walker
Feder
Dellinger
Kuhlwein
Galloway
Cole
Phillipi
Riebel
O'Harra
Wrightsville
Seaman

LOOP #6

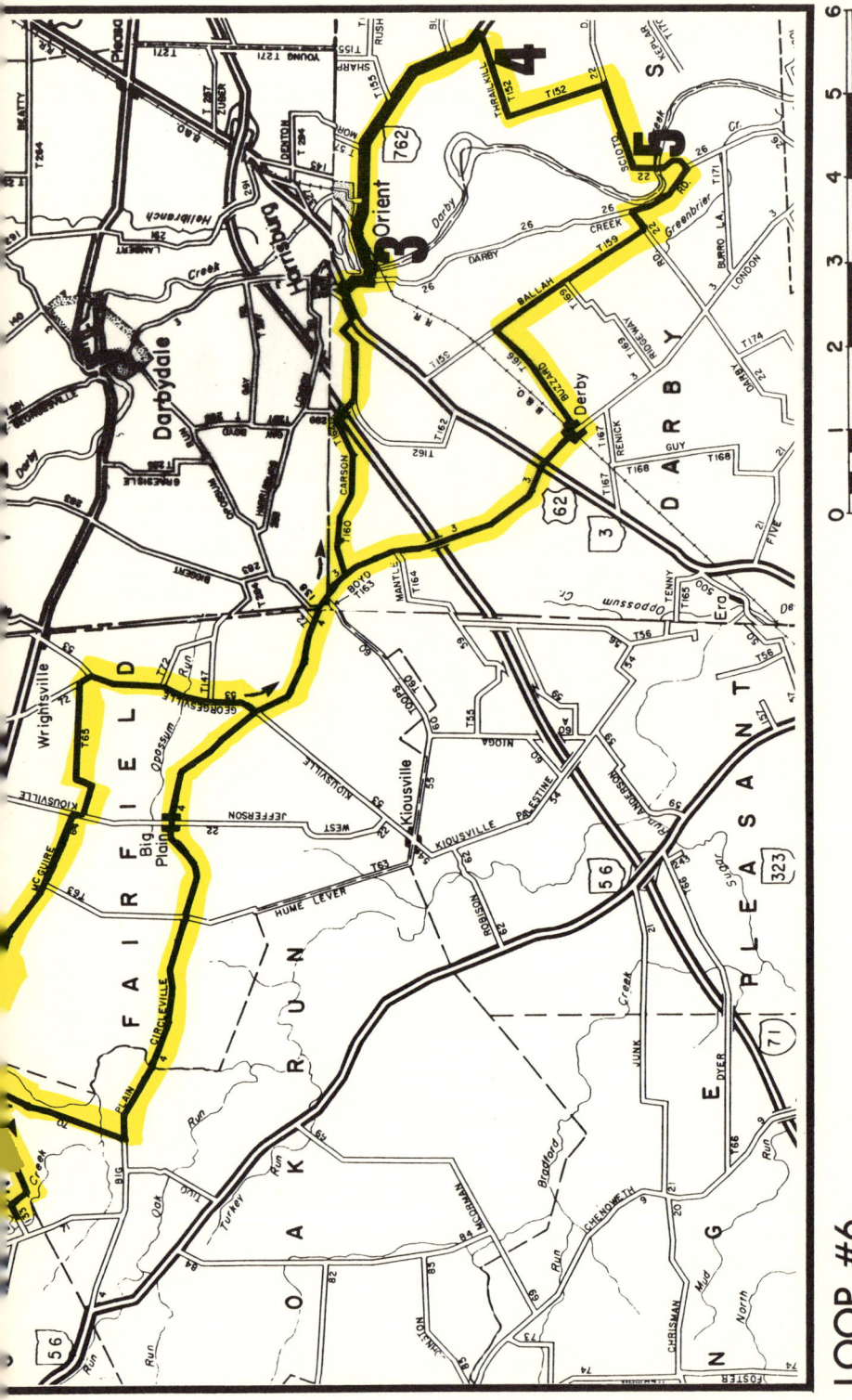

LOOP #7

Distance: 49 miles

Terrain: Flat with a few small hills at the beginning

County: Delaware/Marion/Union

Treaty Line Ride

This ride has long been one of our favorites, and we have enjoyed it in all seasons. It is a very flat ride with almost no traffic, and in some places these country lanes are no wider than driveways. The ride winds along a scenic stretch of the Scioto River before heading into open farmland. Birdlife is abundant along the river, and includes red-headed woodpeckers, kingfishers, bluebirds, flickers, ducks, geese, and more. Turtles can be seen sunning themselves on rocks in the summertime. Farm animals abound in the countryside, with cows grazing in the pastures and horses frolicking in the corrals.

In addition to being a beautiful ride through the countryside, the ride passes through an area of historic significance. Had you taken this ride in 1795, you would have stayed "safely" within the territory and protection of the United States government, but just barely! Ohio was then part of the Northwest Territory, and General "Mad" Anthony Wayne had just defeated the Indians and supposedly secured the area for settlement, although Tecumseh had something else in mind (see Tecumseh Ride). The treaty signed in Greenville in 1795 designated land north of the Treaty Line as Indian territory, with land south of the line to be open for settlement. With the safety of our time travelers uppermost in mind, this ride goes only as far north as the Greenville Treaty Line (now called Boundary Road), turns and follows it westward for a few miles, then loops southward toward Richwood. The journey touches, but does not enter, Indian Territory. Along the way, the keen-eyed "scout" will spot some old cemeteries, an interesting wooden foot bridge, the oldest church in Delaware County, and several steel truss bridges built around the turn of this century. For the botanically inclined, one of the few stands of white cedar found in Ohio can be seen at the confluence of Mills Creek and the Scioto River.

POINTS OF INTEREST:

1. *Bellpoint School*
   The ride begins at this abandoned schoolhouse just north of State Route 42 on Klondike Road.

2. *The Old Stone Church*
   This historic landmark was built in 1835 of gray limestone. It has been in worship for over 150 years, making it the oldest church in continuous service in Delaware County.

3. *Prospect, Ohio*
   A beautiful 1913 steel bridge spans the Scioto River here. Food and drink can be obtained in Prospect, and you'll pass by an old cemetery and the 1884 school bell as you leave town.

4. *Greenville Treaty Line Marker*

5. *Brown-Tyler Pioneer Cemetery*
   This small cemetery has stones pre-dating the Civil War by twenty years. The graves of Civil War veterans are marked as such.

6. *Richwood Park*
   This community park has a swimming area, picnic tables, and a shelterhouse. Food and drink are available in the town. Leave Richwood via E. Ottawa Street.

7. *Steel Truss Bridge over Bokes Creek*

8. *1914 Steel Truss Bridge over Mill Creek*
   Route Note: The route does not cross over the bridge, but turns left at the foot of the bridge. A beautiful view of the creek is provided from the bridge.

9. *Mills Road Foot Bridge*
   This old abandoned foot bridge spans Mill Creek, but is now closed to foot traffic.

10. *Route Note:* To return to Bellpoint School, make a left turn from Mills Road onto S.R. 257, then a quick right onto Bellpoint Road and across the abandoned bridge over the Scioto River. This bridge is closed to automobile traffic, so if you are driving, turn right from Mills Road onto Rt. 257, then left onto Rt. 42 to cross the river.

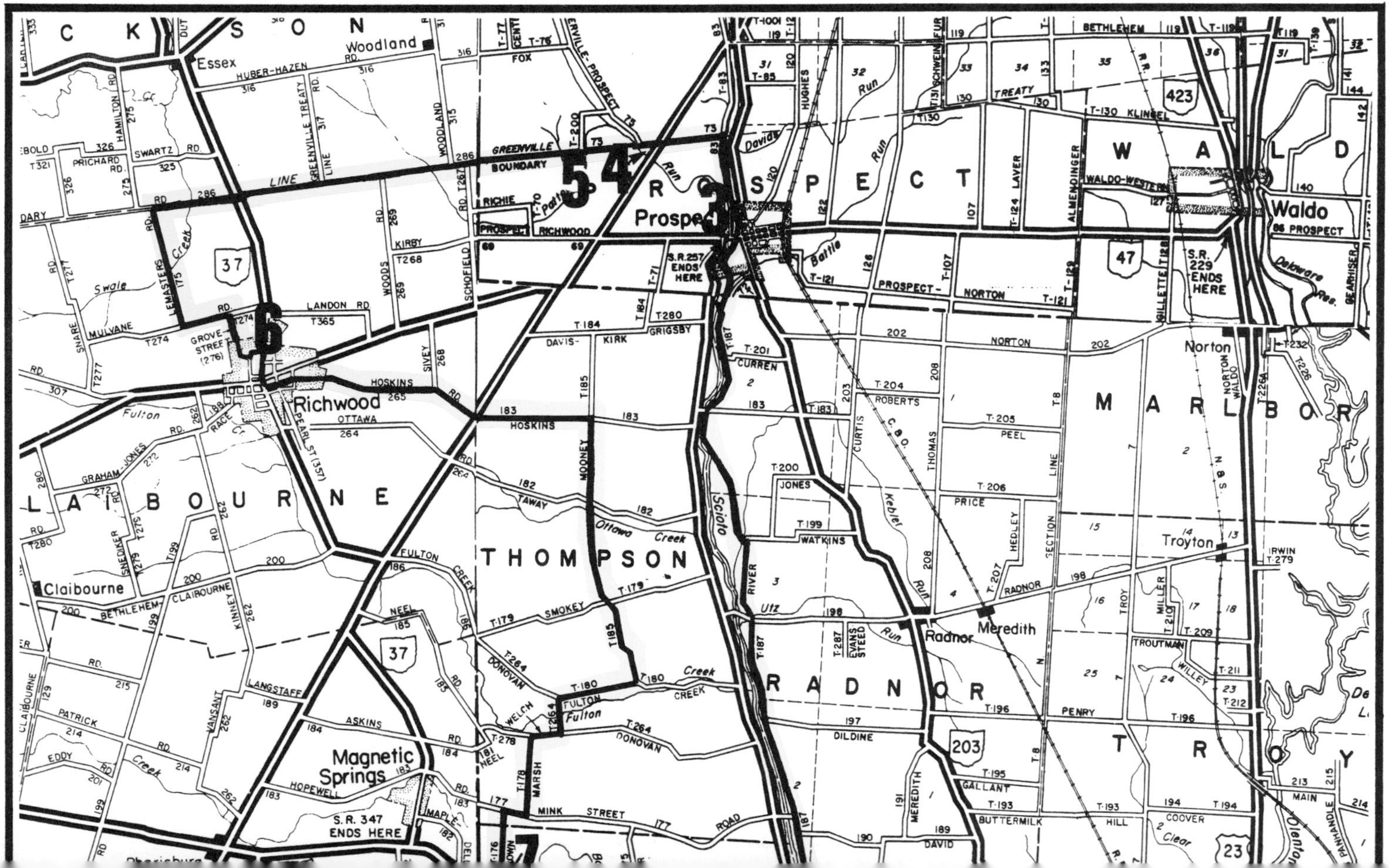

Waldo
Prospect
Richwood
Magnetic Springs
Norton
Troyton
Meredith
Radnor
Claibourne
Essex
Woodland
Scioto
423
47
203
37
23
S.R. 229 ENDS HERE
S.R. 257 ENDS HERE
S.R. 347 ENDS HERE
THOMPSON
RADNOR
PROSPECT
MARLBORO
WALDO

LOOP #7

LOOP #8

Distance: 25 miles

Terrain: Flat with a few small hills at the beginning of the ride

County: Delaware

The Old Stone Church

This is a shortened version of the Treaty Line Ride for those who do not wish to venture so close to the Indian territory of 1795. It cuts the distance of that loop in half, while still offering beautiful scenery and wildlife along the Scioto River and other creeks. The route travels along quiet country roads through open countryside.

One of the dominant features of this ride is the metal truss bridge, and you will encounter no less than three of these splendid structures on this tour. While the wooden covered bridge is still considered the "creme-de-la-creme" by back roads buffs, the metal truss bridge runs a close second. The metal bridge was the most common bridge built between 1875 and 1925. They were considered quite a technological achievement, and are now a reminder of Victorian America. Looking like "erector sets", the chief characteristic of the metal truss bridge is the arrangement of the iron or steel components into the geometrically strong triangle. Unfortunately, the metal truss bridge is beginning to disappear from the landscape, just as its predecessor, the wooden covered bridge, has been doing.

Long before there was a bridge of any kind here, men and women forded the Scioto River on horseback to attend a small stone church which looked over the river from a nearby hill. The pioneers carried their rifles to the worship service for protection from the wild animals as they hiked through the woods to the little church. Today, more than 150 years later, the Old Stone Church, built in 1835, is still in active service. It is the oldest church in continuous worship in Delaware County, and is an interesting feature of this scenic ride.

POINTS OF INTEREST:

1. *Bellpoint School*
   The ride starts at this abandoned schoolhouse just north of State Route 42 on Klondike Road.

2. *The Old Stone Church*

3. *1913 Metal Truss Bridge over the Scioto River*

4. *Metal Truss Bridge over Bokes Creek*

5. *1914 Metal Truss Bridge over Mill Creek*
   Route Note: The route does not cross over this bridge, but turns left at the foot of the bridge.

6. *Mills Road Foot Bridge*
   This old wooden foot bridge crosses Mill Creek, and is now closed to foot traffic.

7. *Route Note:* To return to Bellpoint School, make a left turn onto Route 257 from Mills Road, then a quick right onto Bellpoint Road and across the abandoned bridge. The bridge is closed to automobile traffic, so if you are driving, turn right from Mills Road onto Route 257, then left on Route 42 to cross the river.

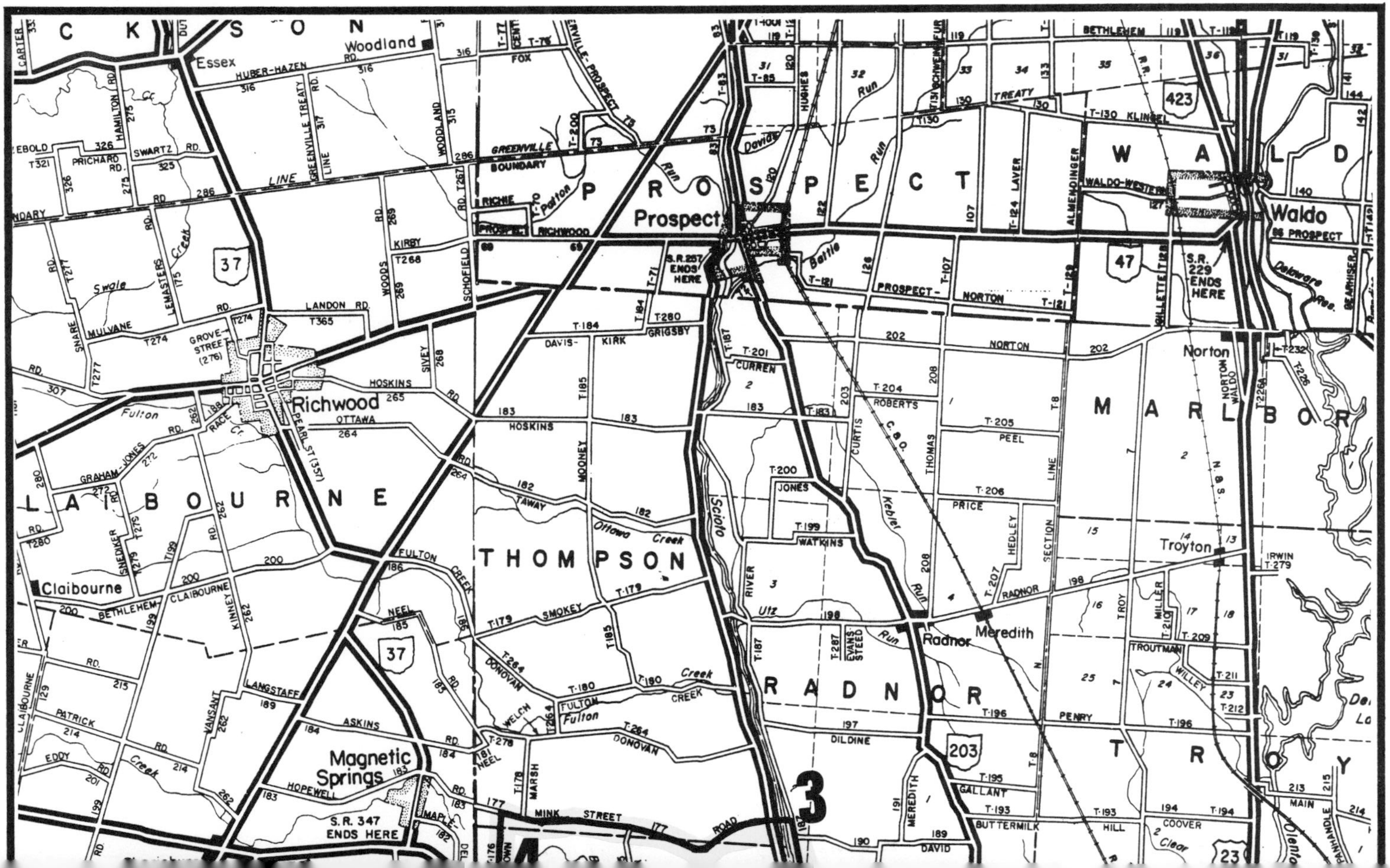

PROSPECT
Prospect
WALDO
Waldo
MARLBORO
Norton
THOMPSON
RADNOR
Radnor
Meredith
Troyton
TROY
CLAIBOURNE
Claibourne
Richwood
Magnetic Springs
Essex
Woodland
S.R. 257 ENDS HERE
S.R. 229 ENDS HERE
S.R. 347 ENDS HERE
Scioto
Delaware Res.
Olentangy
3
4

LOOP #8

LOOP #9

Distance: 46 miles

Terrain: Flat

County: Delaware/Morrow

Books of Stone

This 46 mile ride from Alum Creek State Park leads through level open farmland, crosses an old bowstring bridge, passes by the last covered bridge in Delaware County, and visits four of those history books of stone, the pioneer cemetery.

There are thousands of small pioneer cemeteries scattered throughout Ohio, many with only a handful of graves. These cemeteries tell the story of our state, its settlers, and in large part reflects the history of the new United States. The fact that the earliest cemeteries date back only to the early 1800's is testament to the youthfulness of Ohio, which saw the land opened for settlement after the Greenville Treaty of 1795. Only eight years later, Ohio became the seventeenth state of the Union, and the first state carved from the Northwest Territory. You can trace the history of our nation's early conflicts with a walk through these cemeteries, as the stones mark the final resting place of the soldiers who fought for the principles of the Declaration of Independence in the Revolutionary War; who defended the new country against the British and the Indians of Tecumseh's federation in the War of 1812; and the tragic war that pitted brother against brother, the Civil War, fifty years later. Proportionate to her population, Ohio sent more of her sons to the Union Army than any other state. The stones also tell the story of the migration into Ohio, as settlers poured in from Connecticut, Virginia, Kentucky, and Pennsylvania seeking the freedom and promise of the new land.

History is found not only on the stones, but in the size and location of the cemeteries themselves, as they parallel the development of Ohio. The earliest cemeteries are usually small family plots, with only a handful of graves, located on a piece of high ground on the homestead. In death, as in life, the small group of stones symbolizes the family huddled against a hostile new environment, drawing on itself for support. A short time later, as small communities grew, the church lot became the cemetery for a larger number of families. Eventually, the cemeteries outgrew the church lots, and were located on the outskirts of town, "out of sight, out of mind", according to some.

The artwork and inscriptions on the stones reveal the themes of the ages. Many offer religious inscriptions, with open books and fingers pointing toward heaven; others chastise the living and warn them that "as I am now, so you will be". The willow tree, a symbol of sorrow, adorns many of the earliest stones. The evolution of the material for the markers is also clearly evident, with sandstone being used for the earliest gravestones. Sandstone gave a brown, red, or beige appearance, and its coarse grain made it difficult to inscribe deeply. Therefore, many of these early stones have weathered poorly and are now illegible. White marble or Lithopolis freestone came into use around 1850, and the tablet markers gave way in the 1870's to varied shapes such as tree trunks, pillars, obelisks, and other forms.

The old pioneer cemeteries, although engraved in stone, are a vanishing record of history. Each year, the old stones become more weathered, and more become illegible; some cemeteries disappear altogether, as their stones are broken or lost. But for now, these history books of stone are there for the reading.

POINTS OF INTEREST:

1. *Alum Creek State Park*
   This park offers swimming, picnicking, and camping.

2. *Old Eden-Old Kilbourne Pioneer Cemetery*
   This cemetery has stones dating back to at least 1832.

3. *Stantontown Pioneer Cemetery*
   A memorial to a woman who had been captured by Indians in 1778 and recovered by her father five years later is found here, as are graves of soldiers of the War of 1812 and the Civil War.

4. *1906 Metal Bowstring Bridge over Alum Creek*

5. *Fargo Methodist Episcopal Pioneer Cemetery*
   There are several sandstone markers suitable for rubbings found here, and markers for veterans of the Revolution, the War of 1812, and Civil War are located here.

6. *Chambers Covered Bridge*
   Built in 1874, this is the only remaining covered bridge in Delaware County.

7. *Old Blue Church Cemetery*
   The old church is gone, but the cemetery remains. Stones date back to 1824, and include soldiers of the Revolution, War of 1812, and Civil War. The church bell, cast in 1850, is preserved at the site.

8. *Route Note:* Rough road for about a mile.

9. *Africa, Ohio*
   Settled by William Patterson in 1824, this town was originally named East Orange. A famous stop on the Underground Railroad, the town became known as Africa due to the large number of freed slaves who settled here after the Civil War. The town has now all but disappeared.

NOTES

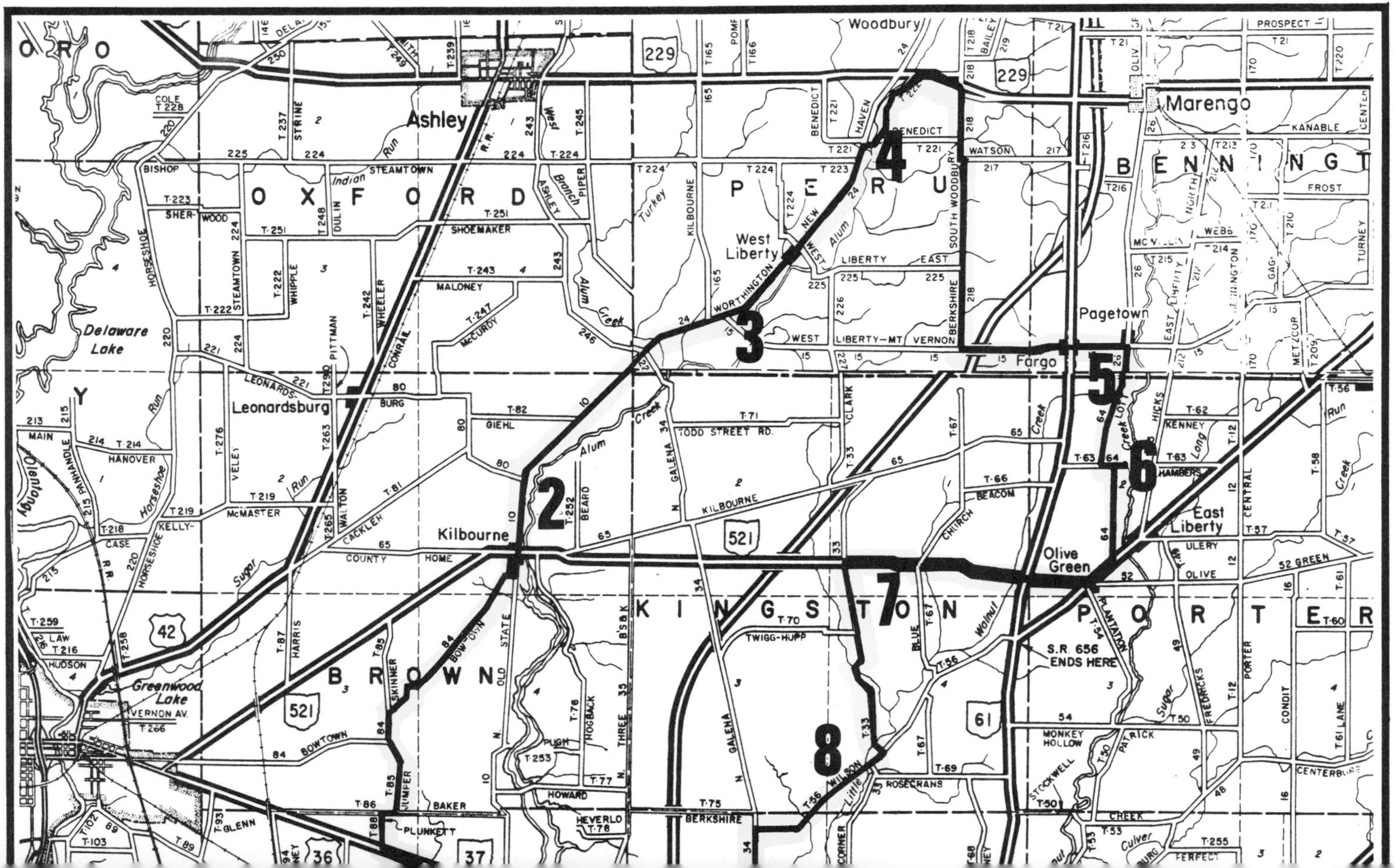
Woodbury
Ashley
Marengo
West Liberty
Pagetown
Fargo
Leonardsburg
Kilbourne
East Liberty
Olive Green
Delaware Lake
Greenwood Lake
O X F O R D
P E R U
B E N N I N G T
K I N G S T O N
P O R T E R
B R O W N
S.R. 656 ENDS HERE
229
42
521
61
36
37
2
3
4
5
6
7
8

LOOP #9

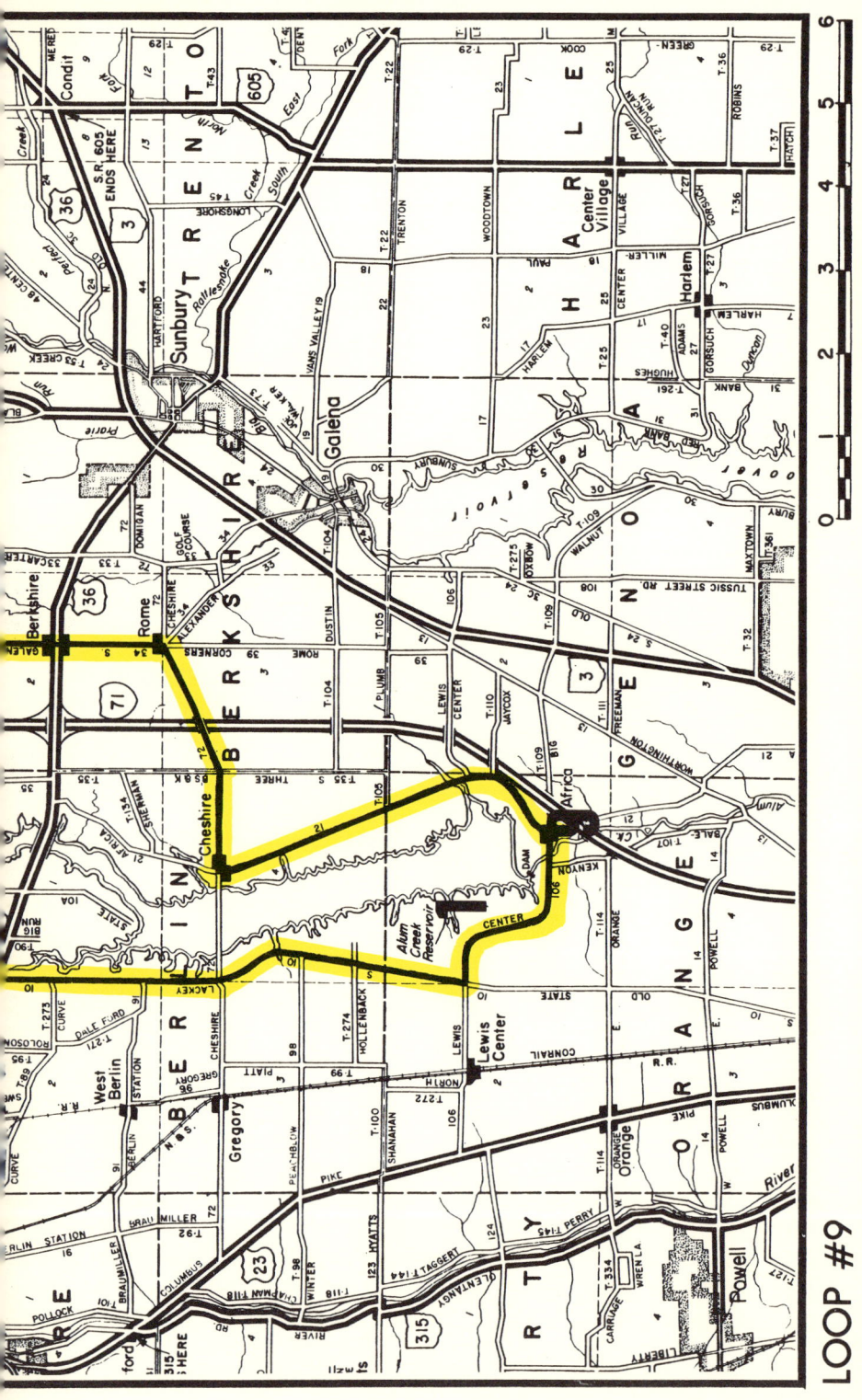

LOOP #10

Distance: 30 miles

Terrain: Mostly flat with a few small hills

County: Pickaway

Slate Run Farm

    The Slate Run Farm Ride, like the Logan Elm Ride, leaves from A.W. Marion State Park, where camping is available. The Slate Run Farm Ride is a 30 mile loop rich in the history of the land and the people who farmed it a century ago. As you ride the ridge top northward, you'll look out over productive farmland and observe modern agriculture at work. Trucks, tractors, combines, and other modern equipment make it possible to farm a much larger area than was dreamed of a century ago. This is a ride of contrasts, because you are traveling back in time to the 1880's, to a farm where the tractors are huge draught horses and the trucks are horse drawn wagons.

    Slate Run Living Historical Farm is not an ordinary farm, but rather an actual working farm using the methods and tools of the 1880's. The farm house was built in 1856 and is still furnished accordingly, and the large red barn was built in 1880. The activities of the farm are always changing, as are the natural rhythms of the seasons and weather. You may see the men and women, in period dress, making soap, butchering, getting the hay in, or tending the farm animals among the myriad chores to be performed.

    From observing people at Slate Run Farm, we go to observing wildlife at Stage's Pond, one of the best spots in the area for observing migrating waterfowl in the spring and fall. Seventeen thousand years ago the glacier covering this area began to recede, and a huge ice chunk broke off and was left behind. The stranded "iceberg" became covered with sand and gravel pouring off the retreating glacier, and when this chunk finally melted after perhaps a millenium, it left a 64 acre depression in the earth. About half of the depression is underwater and forms the kettle lake called Stage's Pond. In addition to the migrating waterfowl that visit the pond, summer residents include great blue herons and other shorebirds. Nearby wooded areas and open fields support songbirds, quail, pheasant, and hawks. A wide variety of wildflowers can be found here from April through October, with the spring being the peak time for color and variety.

POINTS OF INTEREST:

1. *A.W. Marion State Park*
   This park has a 160 acre lake, hiking trails, picnicking, and camping. Cost for camping is $3.00 per night.

2. *Slate Run Living Historical Farm*
   The farm is open daily in the summer except Monday; after Labor Day closed Monday and Tuesday. Operated by the Metropolitan Park District of Columbus and Franklin County, there is an admission charge of $1.75 for adults, students 6-17 $1.25, and children under 6 are free.

3. *Ashville Heritage Museum*
   This little museum is a very friendly and interesting place. The world's first traffic light, which hung in Ashville until only a few years ago, is on display here. The museum is located at 24 Long Street, just one block off the loop in town. Hours: 9-4 Monday through Saturday. Donations accepted.

4. *Stage's Pond Nature Preserve*
   Open year round, dawn to dusk. Water, latrines, an observation blind, and walking trails are provided here.

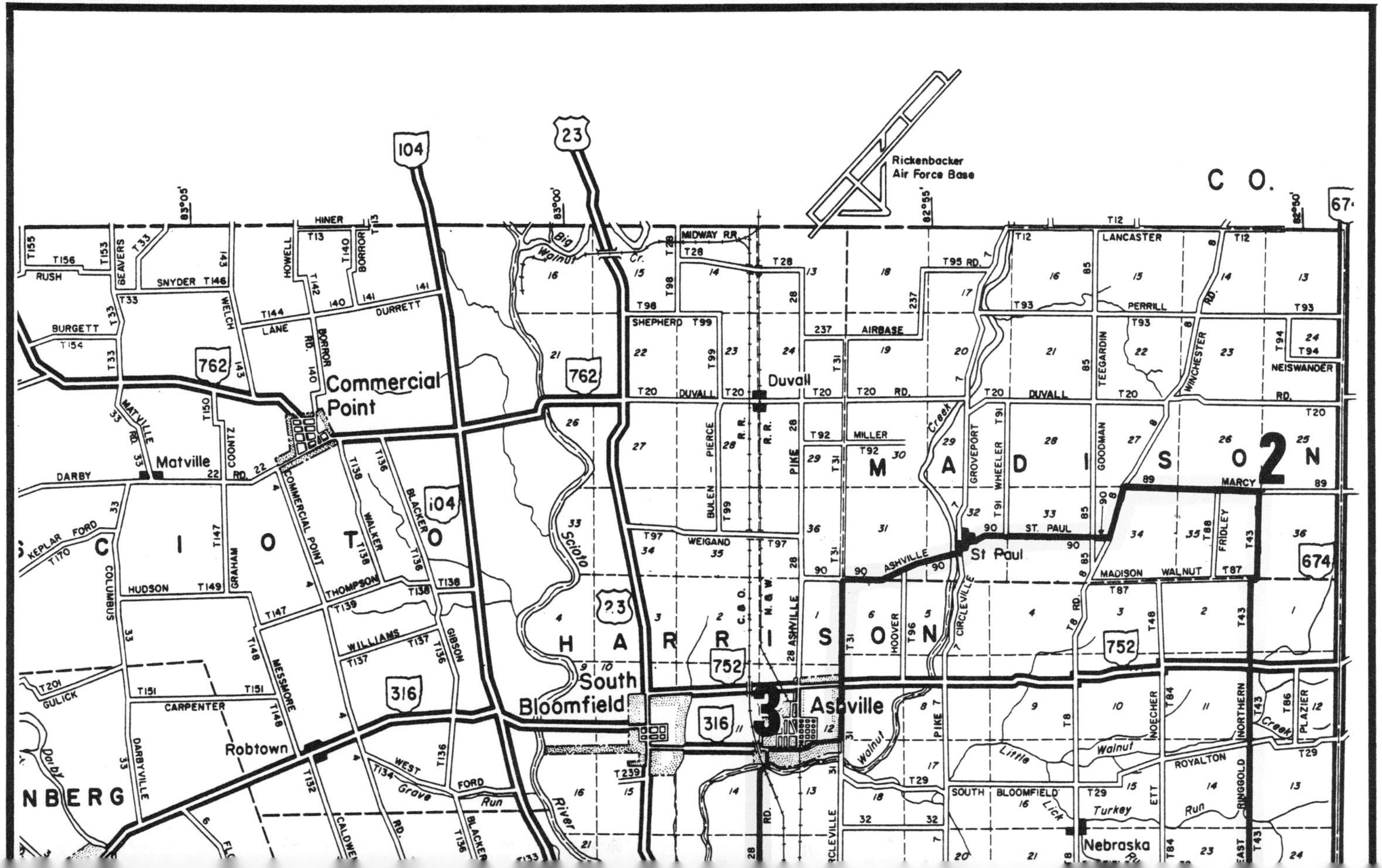

Rickenbacker Air Force Base
CO.
MADISON
HARRISON
SCIOTO
NBERG
Commercial Point
Matville
Duvall
St Paul
South Bloomfield
Ashville
Robtown
Nebraska
Scioto River
Big Walnut Cr.
Walnut Creek
Little Walnut
Little Lick
Turkey Run
Grove Run
Ford Run
Darby
Run
Lick
104
23
762
752
316
674
MIDWAY RR
C. & O.
N. & W.
R.R.
HINER
HOWELL
BORROR
DURRETT
LANE
WELCH
SNYDER T146
BEAVERS
RUSH
BURGETT
COONTZ
MATVILLE RD.
DARBY
KEPLAR FORD
COLUMBUS
HUDSON
GRAHAM
COMMERCIAL POINT
THOMPSON
WALKER
BLACKER
WILLIAMS
GIBSON
MESSMORE
CARPENTER
DARBYVILLE
GULICK
WEST
CALDWELL
SHEPHERD
BULEN - PIERCE
WEIGAND
PIKE
ASHVILLE
AIRBASE
MILLER
DUVALL
GROVEPORT
WHEELER
ST. PAUL
GOODMAN
TEEGARDIN
LANCASTER
PERRILL
WINCHESTER RD.
NEISWANDER RD.
MARCY
FRIDLEY
MADISON
WALNUT
HOOVER
CIRCLEVILLE
T8 RD.
NOECHER
NORTHERN
PLAZIER
ROYALTON
RINGGOLD
EAST
SOUTH BLOOMFIELD
ETT
83°05'
83°00'
82°55'
82°50'

LOOP #10

LOOP #11

Distance: 29 miles

Terrain: Rolling

County: Pickaway

The Logan Elm

This ride, as well as the Slate Run Farm Ride, begins at A.W. Marion State Park near Circleville, providing the opportunity to couple two days of riding with a campout at the park. The route takes you over rolling hills, through beautiful countryside, and offers panoramic views overlooking pastures, ponds, and barns. The site of the Logan Elm, now a state historical site, is the highlight of this trip. This important memorial is located on the Pickaway Plains, an area steeped in history, and commemorates one of the darkest pages in Ohio's past.

The recorded history of Pickaway County began in 1774 when Lord Dunmore led an army into the Ohio Valley to wage war against the Indians. Shawnee leaders tried to persuade the Mingo chief, Tay-ga-yee-ta, known as Logan on the frontier, to join them in battling the militia. Chief Logan, however, was a man of peace, known to the Indians and whites alike as a warm and friendly person. He had, in fact, served as a peacemaker in previous conflicts, including the French and Indian War. He was welcomed in various tribal houses and settler's homes, for he was considered most trustworthy. As one grizzled old frontiersman said, "Logan is the best specimen of humanity I ever met with, either white or red." Logan refused the pleas of the Shawnees to take up arms against Dunmore, counseling instead for peace and negotiation. But only a few weeks later, while Logan was away, his family was viciously murdered by a party of men led by Jacob Greathouse, who posed as friends and lured the Indians into their camp for games and drink. Upon finding his family murdered, the chief no longer sought peace, but rather sought revenge. When the fighting ended, General Dunmore had won the war, but Logan refused to join the other Indian leaders at the treaty signing with the general. Instead, he dictated a message beneath a spreading elm tree to be read for him at the meeting. Although he mistakenly accused Colonel Cresap for his family's murder, the speech is one of the most eloquent ever delivered, and has been translated into almost every language. The tree under which he gave the speech came to be known as Logan's Elm.

The magnificent elm tree, with a span of more than 120 feet and height of 100 feet, fell victim to Dutch Elm disease nearly two centuries later in 1964, but the spot continues to be a state memorial commemorating not only Logan, but other Indian leaders as well. The chief's moving speech has been engraved in marble at the site, and you can also observe a touching footnote placed at the base of a marker by schoolchildren in 1980, closing this sad chapter more than 200 years later.

POINTS OF INTEREST:

1. *A.W. Marion State Park*
   This park has a 160 acre lake, hiking trails, picnicking, and camping. The camping fee is $3.00 per night.

2. *Logan Elm Historical Site*
   The memorial is operated by the Ohio Historical Society, and is open daily.

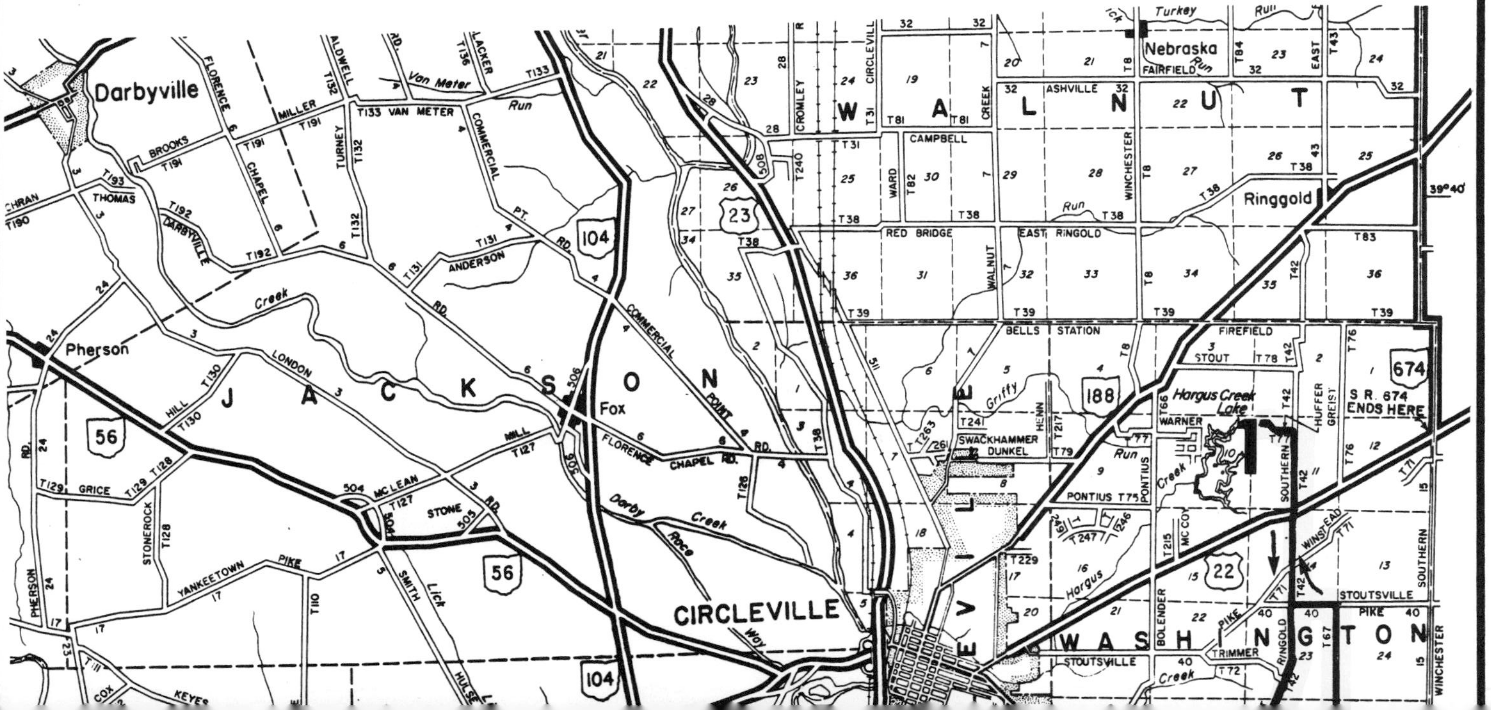

Darbyville
Pherson
Fox
CIRCLEVILLE
Nebraska
Ringgold
W A L N U T
J A C K S O N
W A S H I N G T O N
Hargus Creek Lake
S R. 674 ENDS HERE
39°40'
674
188
104
23
56
22
Darby Creek
Turkey Run
Van Meter Run
Hargus Creek
Griffy Run
Lick
COMMERCIAL PT. RD.
FLORENCE CHAPEL RD.
LONDON
YANKEETOWN PIKE
STONEROCK
GRICE
HILL
MC LEAN
STONE
SMITH
HULSE
MILL
ANDERSON
TURNEY
VAN METER
MILLER
BROOKS
THOMAS
DARBYVILLE
CHAPEL
CROMLEY
CIRCLEVILL
CAMPBELL
WARD
RED BRIDGE
WALNUT
EAST RINGOLD
WINCHESTER
ASHVILLE
FAIRFIELD
EAST
BELLS STATION
FIREFIELD
STOUT
WARNER
HUFFER
GREIST
SOUTHERN
SWACKHAMMER
DUNKEL
HENN
PONTIUS
MC COY
BOLENDER
STOUTSVILLE
TRIMMER
RINGOLD
PIKE
WINSTEAD
KEYES
COX

LOOP #11

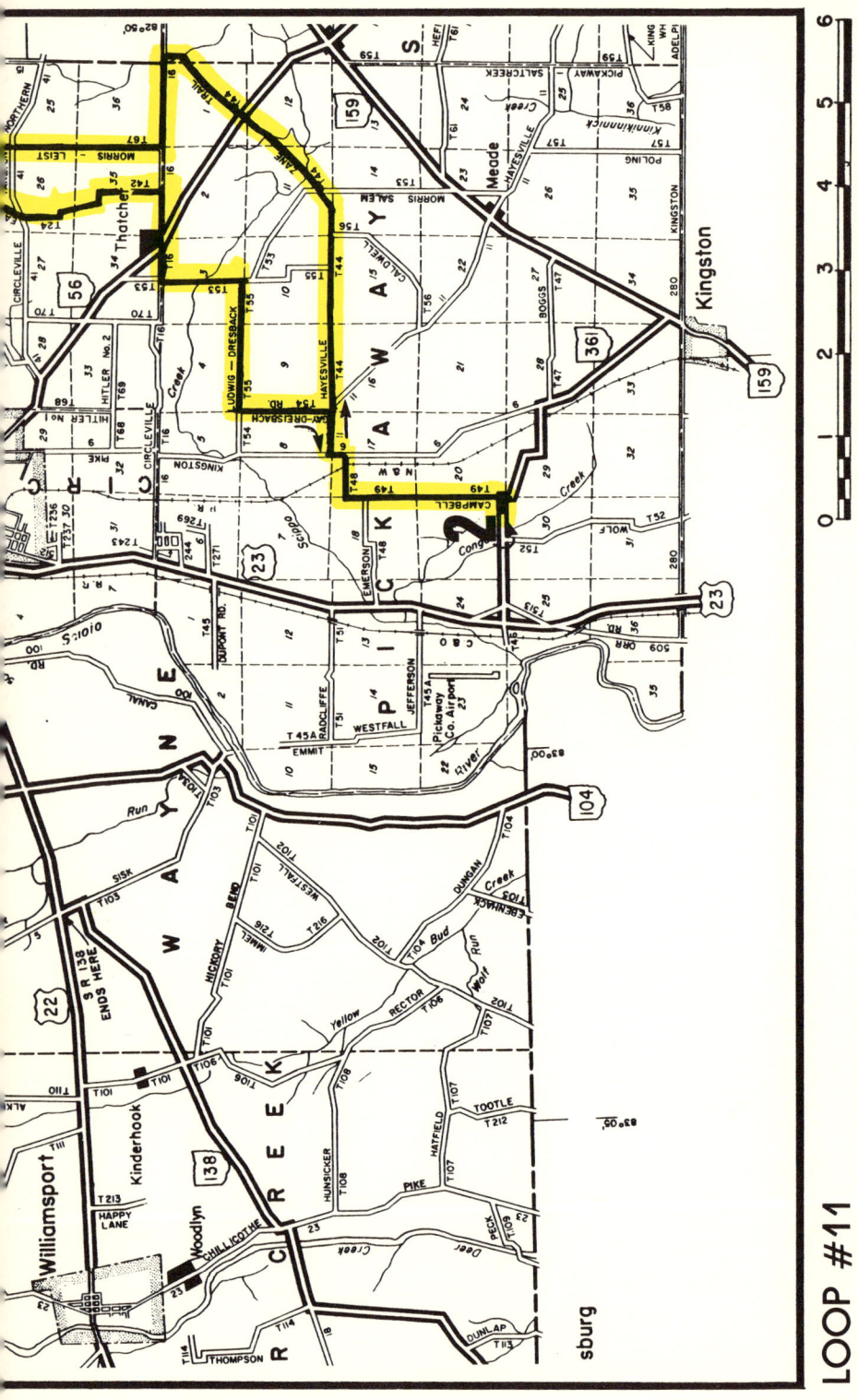

LOOP #12

Distance: 34 miles

Terrain: First half rather hilly, second half flatter

County: Fairfield

The Glacier's Edge

This ride from Lithopolis takes you over rolling hills and through broad valleys, past a covered bridge, a nature preserve, and an unusual old cemetery. It is, indeed, a very beautiful ride, and owes part of its beauty to the master sculptor of thousands of years ago, the glacier. You are entering the edge of the foothills of the Appalachian Plateau, and are riding terrain where the glacier made its furthest advance before stopping just beyond the southern edge of this loop. The 1,000 foot high ice sheet left behind deposits that covered over the previously eroded landscape, filling and broadening valleys, smoothing hilltops, reversing streams, and creating a more rolling topography than the hilly terrain just to the south. In addition to the glacier's broad strokes, its fine-brush artistry can also be seen on this loop. Looking north from the covered bridge at Rock Mill, you will see a narrow gorge carved in the resistant blackhand sandstone by a tremendous volume of water rushing through here from a draining glacial lake 17,000 years ago. Below the bridge is a huge pothole that was created by the swirling motion of the water carrying sand and pebbles, which scoured into the less resistant sandstone there. The old covered bridge spanning the gorge makes this one of the most picturesque spots anywhere.

Another interesting feature found on this ride is the Stonewall Cemetery. This unusual cemetery, dated 1817, has about a dozen gravestones inside an eight foot high circular wall of sandstone blocks. The stones are pre-1850, and one marks the resting place of a young boy "who was removed from time to eternity by the fall of a tree which instantly deprived him of life." An iron gate on the far side of the wall provides a view within.

The first half of the ride is rather hilly, with the return portion considerably flatter. Therefore, a clockwise direction of travel is recommended. An extended version of this ride, the Old Wooden Bridge Ride, is found in this book, and takes you beyond the southern boundary of this ride.

POINTS OF INTEREST:

1. *Wagnall's Memorial*
   Three public libraries and a community center are housed in this ornate Tudor/Gothic stone building at 150 E. Columbus Street. Open daily.

2. *Rock Mill Covered Bridge and Mill*
   The old mill, built in 1824, has been used as a barn since 1906, and is on private property. The covered bridge, spanning the headwaters of the Hocking River, was built in 1849.

3. *Shallenberger State Nature Preserve*
   We watched a great blue heron flying along the stream at this undeveloped preserve ¼ mile from Crumley Road.

4. *Stonewall Cemetery*

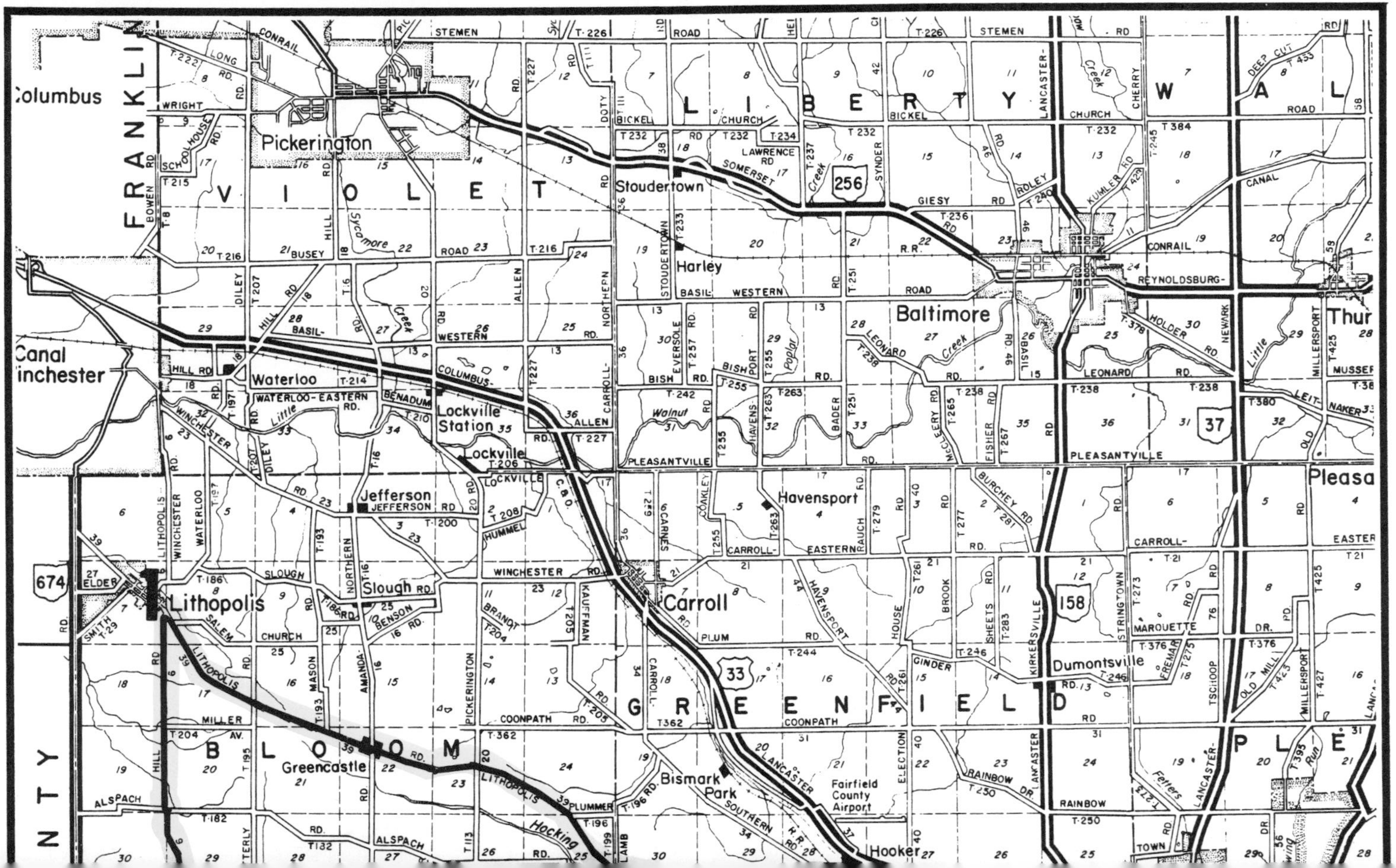

Columbus
FRANKLIN
Pickerington
VIOLET
LIBERTY
WALNUT
Stoudertown
Harley
Baltimore
Thur
Canal Winchester
Waterloo
Lockville Station
Lockville
Jefferson
Havensport
Pleasa
Lithopolis
Slough
Carroll
Dumontsville
GREENFIELD
BLOOM
Greencastle
Bismark Park
Fairfield County Airport
Hooker
PLE
NTY
256
37
158
33
674

LOOP #12

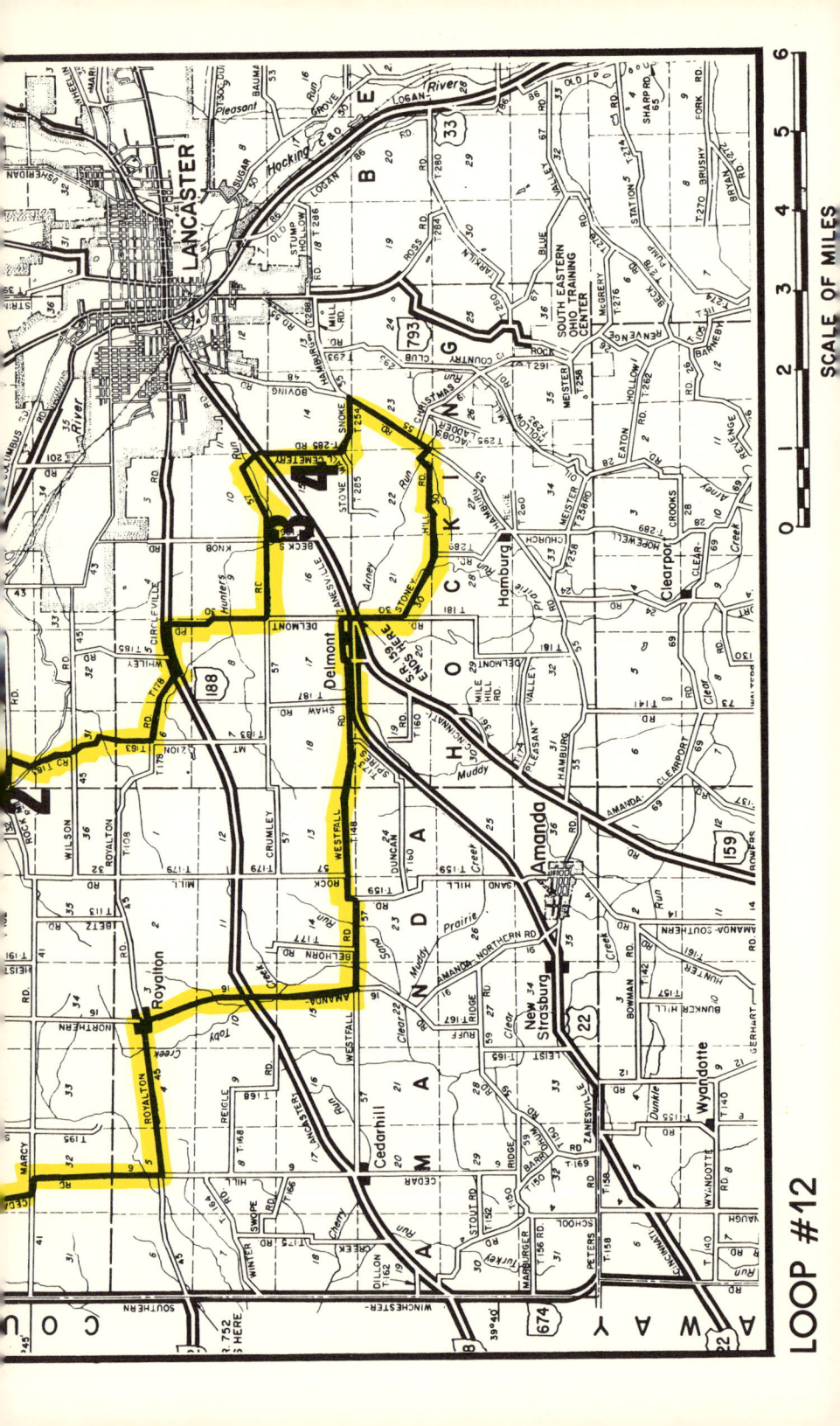

LOOP #13

Distance: 49 miles

Terrain: First half rather hilly, second half flatter

County: Fairfield

The Old Wooden Bridge Ride

This enchanting ride is an extended version of the Glacier's Edge Ride, designed for those adventurers who wish to continue beyond the rolling countryside into the steeper hills lying to the south. The traveler on this route will cross the line of the glacier's furthest advance in Ohio, and see terrain that may have typified much of Ohio before the first glacier crept over the state millions of years ago. The increased effort demanded by the hills is doubly rewarded by magnificent views of tree covered slopes and stream carved valleys, and more of those romantic reminders of our rural past, the covered bridge. All this combines to make this one of the most beautiful rides in the book.

This loop has three covered bridges in all, and also one of its successors, the steel truss bridge, itself becoming an endangered species. The first covered bridge in Ohio was built in 1817, and thousands more followed throughout that century. The covered bridge helped speed the settling of Ohio by providing a less expensive and time consuming alternative to the laborious stone bridges of that era. Fairfield County has held the national record for most covered bridges in one county, topping all the counties of New England. That any of these structures still stands more than 100 years later is testament to the pioneers' strength and endurance. Sadly, all things must eventually pass, and these nostalgic old bridges are fast disappearing from the scene.

Why are covered bridges covered? The primary reason is to protect the trusses of the bridge from the weather. One official long ago wrote, "The plan of leaving bridges uncovered has not provided good economy with us. Six years is the utmost limit that a due regard for safety will permit their use, if uncovered; while they might be trusted for a much longer time if properly protected from the weather." Once erected, though, the bridges served other purposes, including providing a "sparking" place for buggy riders, thereby giving the bridges the nickname of "hugging bridge". There were even claims that the bridges were made to look like barns to fool the horses into crossing streams that they otherwise might have resisted.

Nearly all the covered bridges in Ohio have been victimized by graffiti, but this is hardly a new phenomenon. In the days when the bridges were new, they were plastered with posters hawking patent medicine cures, and, of course, election time saw the plethora of political posters adorning the sides of the bridges. These old bridges truly harken back to our past, so as you travel these back roads of Fairfield County and cross clear creeks gurgling beneath the bridges, listen carefully. Perhaps you will hear the echoes of the shod hooves of horses clip-clopping on the rattling boards; or perhaps hear the drumming of the raindrops on the roof as farmers waited out a sudden summer storm in the shelter of the bridge; or smell the hay and straw of the carts passing through, heading for the daylight framed at bridge's end.

As you enjoy these covered bridges on the southern edge of this ride, take heart that you can also look forward to much flatter terrain on your way back to Lithopolis.

POINTS OF INTEREST:

1. *Wagnall's Memorial*
   Three public libraries and a community center are housed in this ornate Tudor/Gothic stone building at 150 E. Columbus Street. Open daily.

2. *Rock Mill Covered Bridge and Mill*
   This covered bridge, built in 1849, spans a beautiful gorge over the headwaters of the Hocking River. Rock Mill, built in 1824, stands nearby, and has been used as a barn since 1906. The mill is on private property.

3. *Shallenberger State Nature Preserve*
   This undeveloped nature preserve is located about ¼ mile from Crumley Road. There are no facilities here, but you may catch a glimpse of a great blue heron flying along the little stream that winds through the field.

4. *Stonewall Cemetery*
   This small, unusual cemetery, dated 1817, has about a dozen gravestones inside an eight-foot high circular wall of sandstone blocks.

5. *Jacob's Ladder*
   This dead-end gravel road leads through a beautiful valley past a "hog-back" of Blackhand sandstone with seams appearing like rungs on a ladder. This towering rock face seems to reach the sky, hence its name.

6. *Route Note*
   Here the route passes along the grounds of the Southern Ohio Training Center, a correctional institution. Bear to the right at the top of the hill, and follow County Road 26 through the area.

7. *Barneby Nature Center*
   The E.E. Good Prairie can be found at the top of the hill by the entrance. The road to Barneby crosses over a steel truss bridge.

8. *Johnson Covered Bridge*
   This bridge, probably built in the 1870's, spans Clear Creek. Due to the sharp curves in the road, the sides are open to provide better visibility. The bridge uses the Howe truss design.

9. *George Hutchins Covered Bridge*
   Named after the owner of the property when the bridge was built, the structure is located just to the left of the route on Strickler Road. This bridge was also probably built in the 1870's.

NOTES

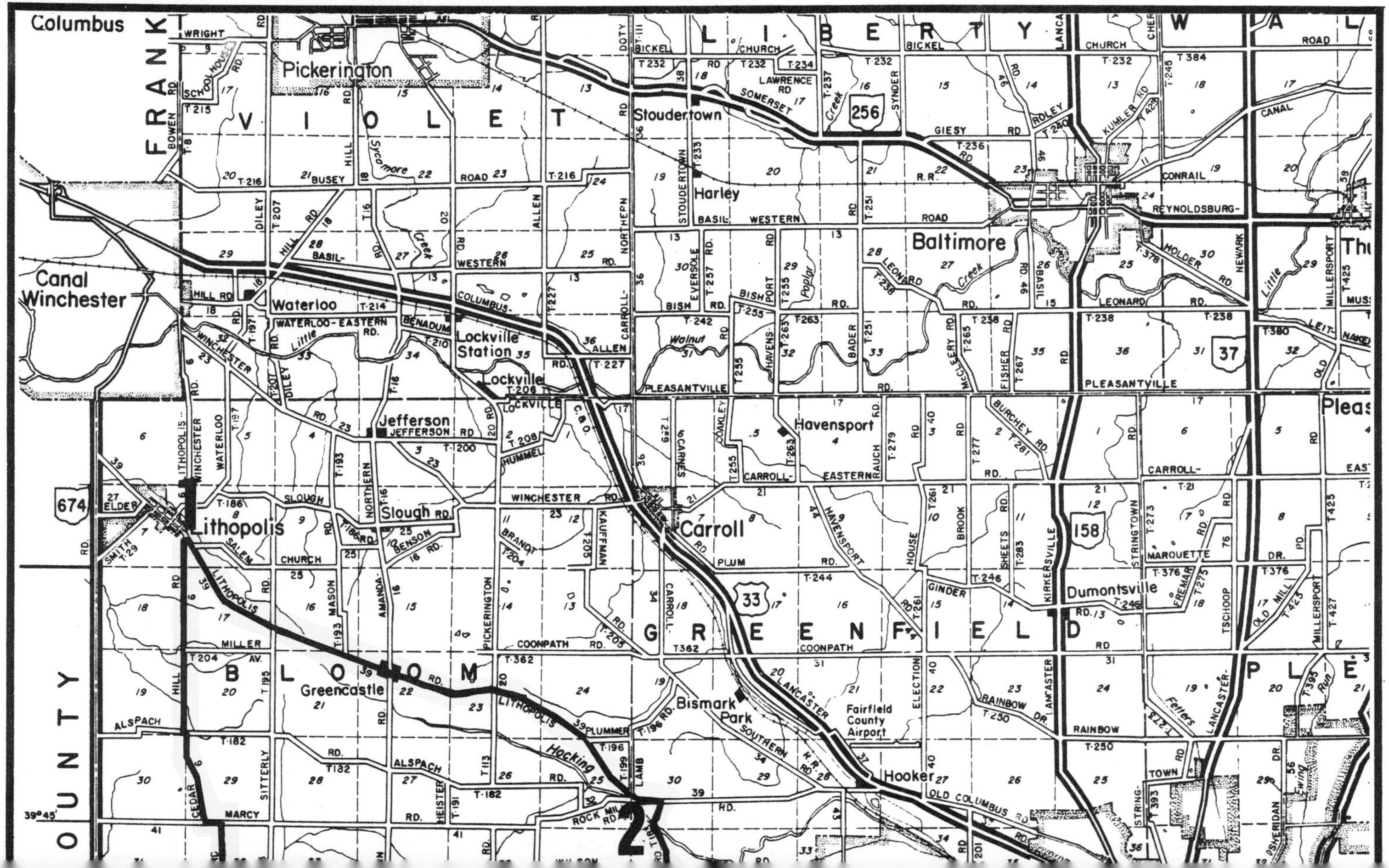

Columbus
FRANK
VIOLET
LIBERTY
GREENFIELD
BLOOM
COUNTY
Pickerington
Stoudertown
Harley
Baltimore
Canal Winchester
Waterloo
Lockville Station
Lockville
Jefferson
Slough
Lithopolis
Havensport
Carroll
Dumontsville
Greencastle
Bismark Park
Fairfield County Airport
Hooker
256
37
158
33
674
39°45'

LOOP #13

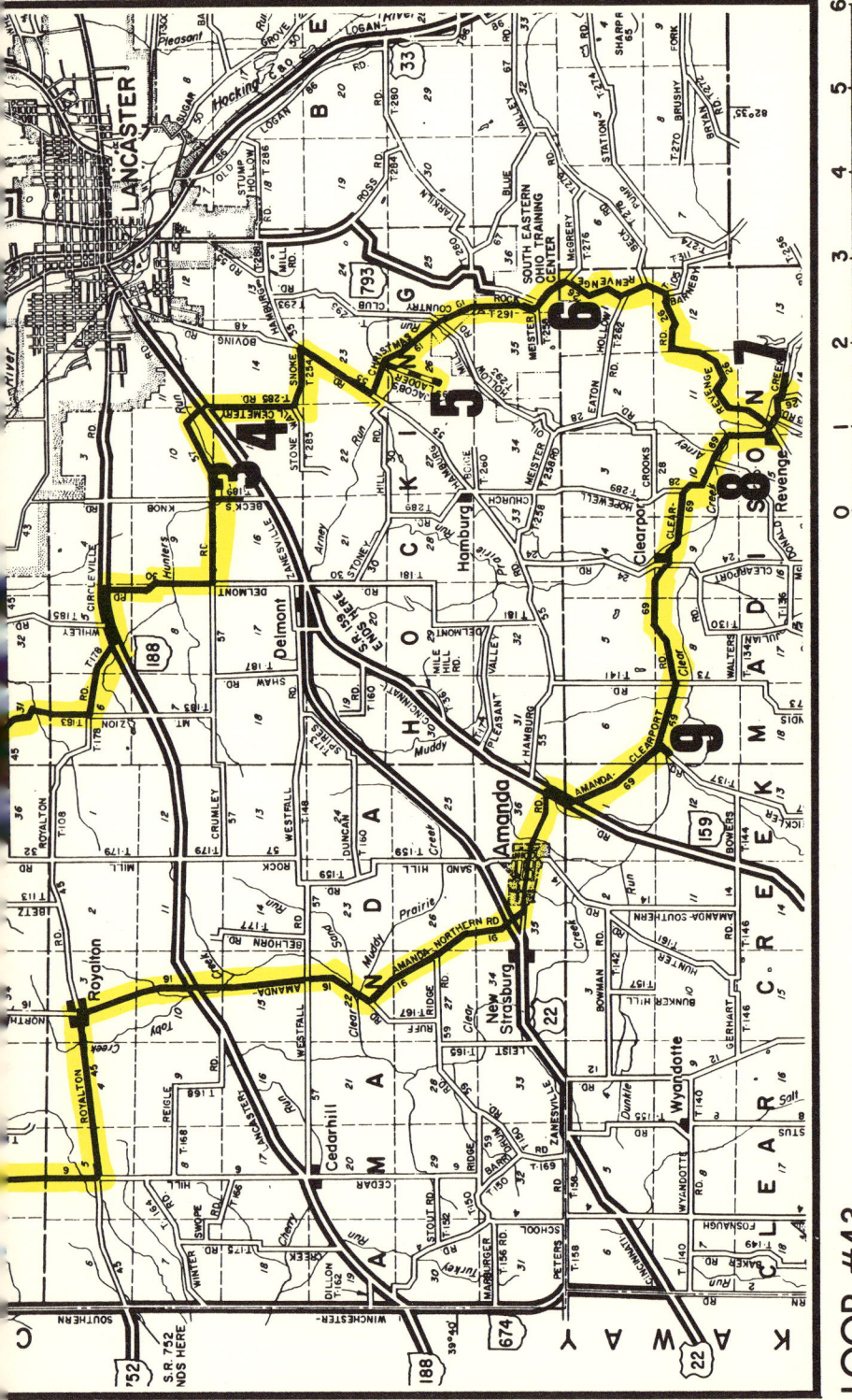

LOOP #14

Distance: 40 miles

Terrain: Gently rolling with some steep hills

County: Licking

The Arboretum Ride

    This ride combines nature and history in one stop at magnificent Dawes Arboretum. You will ride from Alexandria over some fairly steep hills into flatter open country, along fencerows so close to the winding lane that you can almost reach out and touch the cows as they graze in the pastures. You'll rattle across the Licking River on an old steel bridge with wooden floorboards as you meander towards the arboretum.

    Ohio has an extensive and varied flora, with thousands of different species of trees and shrubs found here. The interest in native plants of Ohio extends all the way back to 1788, when the newly opened area was part of the Northwest Territory. A man named Dr. Manasseh Cutler, after stopping in Philadelphia to discuss botanical interests with Benjamin Franklin, headed down the Ohio River to compile a record of native plant life. He dreamed of creating a botanical garden, but in those rugged days of the Ohio frontier, such a dream was unlikely to be fulfilled anytime soon. However, the idea persisted through the centuries, and in 1917 Beman Gates Dawes, great-great-grandson of Manasseh Cutler, made the first horticultural planting at what is now Dawes Arboretum. In 1927, the first tree was dedicated, and the second one was dedicated by Charles Gates Dawes, then Vice-President of the United States. More dedications have followed at the arboretum by latter-day Ohio pioneers such as Orville Wright and John Glenn. Today, more than 2,000 species of trees and shrubs are found on the 950 acres of the arboretum, ranging from the oaks and maples to a bald cypress swamp; white paper birches and tall pines; azalea glens and dogwoods, and a fascinating grove of holly trees. Thousands of plant specimens are clearly labeled along the trails that lead through the grounds. An enchanting Japanese garden, complete with a tranquil pond, provides a perfect spot for meditation and reflection. As you roam the grounds, you may also come upon a small hillside cemetery.

Nestling at wood's edge, the cemetery has stones dating back to 1812, and serves as the final resting place for several Revolutionary War soldiers. A replica of a log cabin stands nearby.

The return ride to Alexandria includes a stop in the old town of Granville, often described as one of the prettiest in Ohio. Historic inns, including the Buxton Inn, built in 1812, are found here, as well as many small shops, an ice cream parlor, and museum. The route from Granville continues along a back road, with an alternative of a bike path available for cyclists. This alternative requires much caution, however, and is not recommended due to the number of pedestrians using the path, especially on weekends.

To lengthen your ride to include Flint Ridge, see the Flint Ridge Ride for a connecting route.

POINTS OF INTEREST:

1. *Alexandria*
   The ride begins here, and there is a public parking lot near the center of town.

2. *Gaffield Pioneer Cemetery*

3. *Steel Truss Bridge*

4. *Route Note:* The road surface becomes packed gravel for about ½ mile.

5. *Dawes Arboretum*
   Located on Route 13, facilities at the arboretum include picnic tables, a shelterhouse, hiking trails, library and gift shop. Open until dark, there is no admission charge.

6. *Granville, Ohio*
   Established in 1805, the town boasts several historic buildings, including the Buxton Inn, located at 313 E. Broadway.

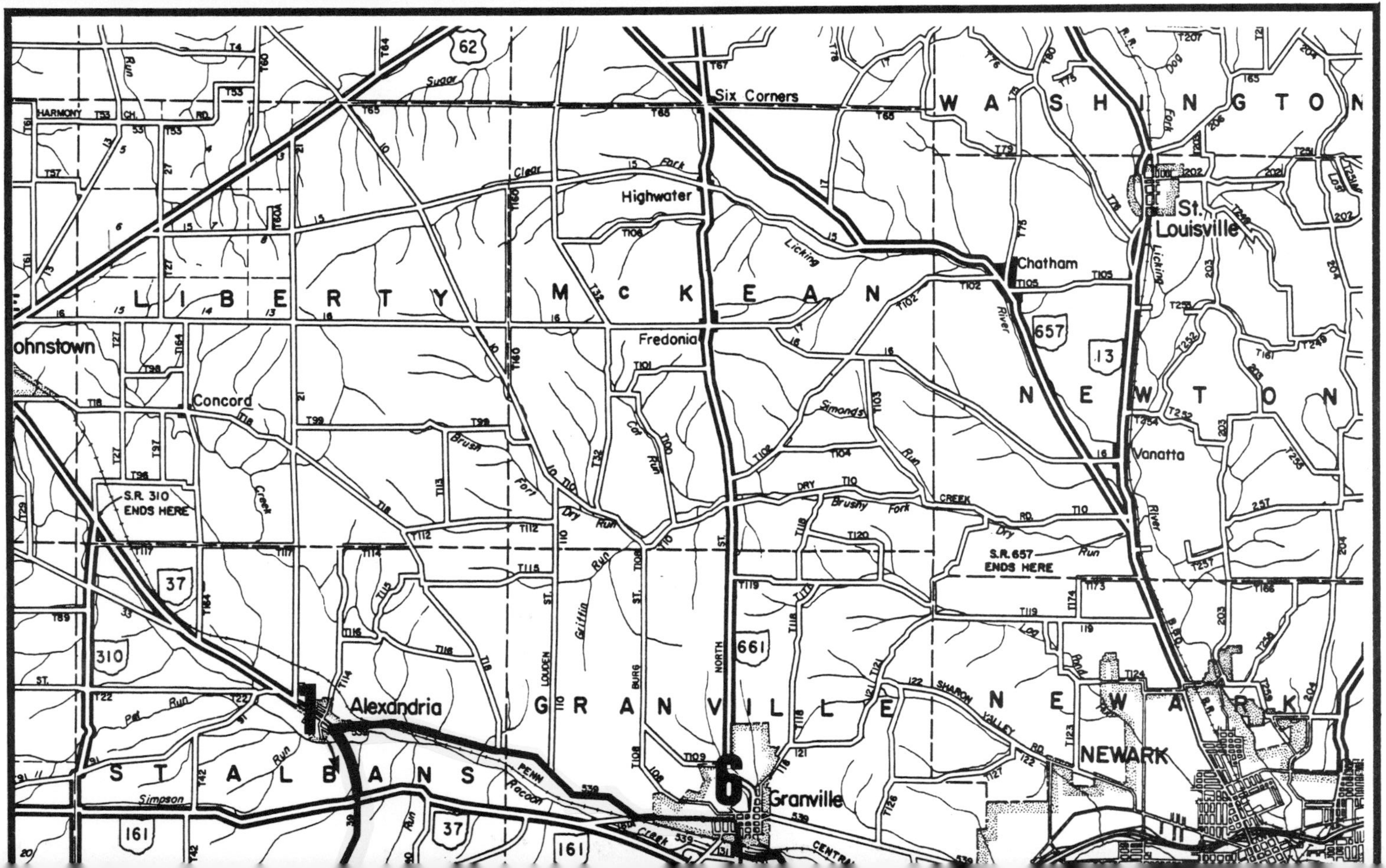

WASHINGTON
LIBERTY
McKEAN
NEWTON
GRANVILLE
NEWARK
ST. ALBANS
Six Corners
Highwater
Chatham
St. Louisville
Fredonia
Johnstown
Concord
Vanatta
Alexandria
Granville
NEWARK
S.R. 310 ENDS HERE
S.R. 657 ENDS HERE
HARMONY CH. RD.
SHARON VALLEY RD.
DRY CREEK RD.
LOUDEN ST.
BURG ST.
NORTH ST.
Licking River
Clear Fork
Brushy Fork
Dry Run
Simonds Run
Cat Run
Griffin Run
Log Pond
Racoon Creek
Simpson
Sugar
62
657
13
661
6
37
310
161
539

LOOP #14

LOOP #15

Distance: 20 miles

Terrain: Hilly

County: Licking

Flint Ridge Ride

This ride can begin at either Flint Ridge Memorial or Black Hand Gorge Nature Preserve. The roads connecting these two beautiful historic sites are hilly, and one section is hard packed dirt with some gravel, making this a ride for experienced cyclists. The views this ride affords are quite beautiful, and worth the effort to the adventurous rider. You can start the ride at one site and tour to the other for a picnic, as tables are provided at both.

Flint has played a major role in both the natural history of the land now called Ohio and the history of its people. This ride to Flint Ridge graphically demonstrates to the cyclist (by sight and muscle strain) the impact of flint. The gemstone was such an important commodity to the early Indians that this area was considered neutral territory and accessible to all. Indians traveled great distances to this five-square mile area to acquire flint, which was used to make tools for fire-making and weapons. Here is found the highest quality flint in the Midwest, and implements made from Flint Ridge flint have been found a thousand miles away.

This layer of hard flint also had another impact on the area, as you know from experience if you biked/hiked up the hill to the ridge. This hard flint serves as the capstone for this ridge, making it highly resistant to erosion. The surrounding countryside, suffering the effects of erosion, has "fallen" in relation to Flint Ridge, thereby creating the hills you have climbed to reach the memorial. The magnificent views on this ride are, in part, a result of the erosion-resistant flint. Flint has played such a key role that it is now the official gemstone of Ohio.

The nearby Black Hand Gorge bears a historic link to Flint Ridge beyond the fact that they are both now nature preserves. Because of the flint at Flint Ridge, the Licking River became a key transportation link for Indians journeying to Flint Ridge to obtain the stone. You will be retracing that journey, in part, on this ride.

The most significant natural feature of Black Hand Gorge is the narrow gorge cut by the Licking River through the blackhand sandstone found here. The name "blackhand" derives from a large dark hand-shaped symbol that once overlooked the gorge from a cliff face. One Indian legend has it that the hand represented sacred Indian territory where no man was to lift his hand against another. The figure was destroyed in 1828 by workmen dynamiting the cliff face to make way for the Ohio-Erie Canal towpath. The remains of the canal locks, and the trolley tunnels that came later, can still be found in the preserve.

POINTS OF INTEREST:

1. *Flint Ridge State Memorial*
   Operated by the Ohio Historical Society, the memorial has hiking trails, a nature preserve, picnic tables, and a museum containing Indian tools and artifacts. An interesting three-dimensional layout of the topography of the area is also on display. The museum is open in the summer Weds.-Sun., weekends in the fall, and closed in the winter. There is an admission charge of $1.50.

2. *Route Note:* This road is hard packed dirt with some gravel.

3. *Black Hand Gorge State Nature Preserve*
   This preserve is maintained by the Ohio Department of Natural Resources, and is open year round during daylight hours. Picnic tables and hiking trails are provided. *Route Note:* The route through the preserve is a 4.5 mile bike path, and is quite hazardous for cyclists due to joggers, baby carriages, dogs, children, etc. Be careful! (Cars may select another route from the map.)

4. *Dawes Arboretum (Side Trip)*
   If you wish to extend the ride to Dawes, follow the dashed lines on the map. A description of the arboretum is provided in the text of the Dawes Arboretum Ride. This scenic extension would add about 20 miles to the ride.

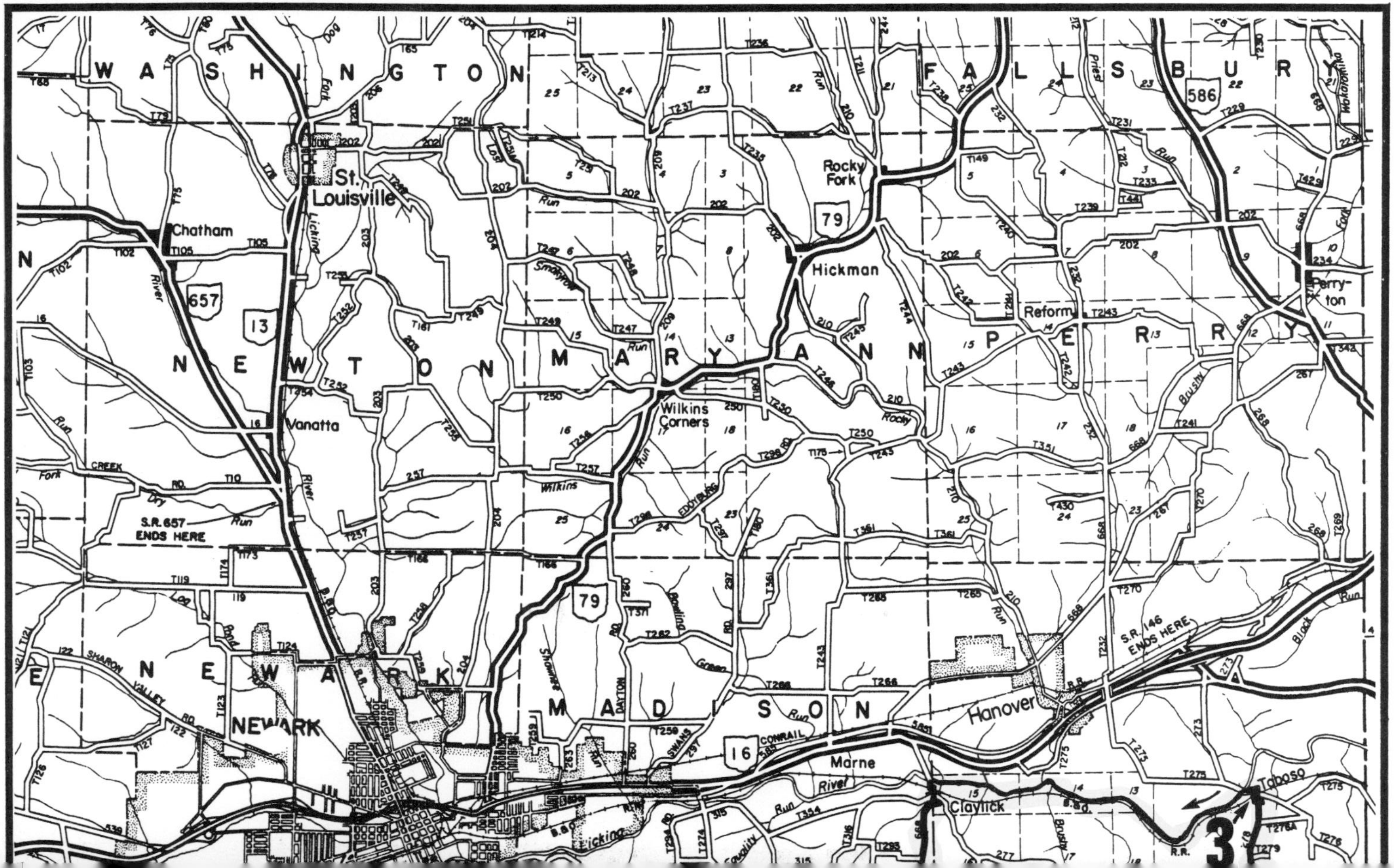
WASHINGTON
FALLSBURY
NEWTON
MARY ANN
PERRY
NEWARK
MADISON
St. Louisville
Chatham
Vanatta
Rocky Fork
Hickman
Reform
Perry-ton
Wilkins Corners
Hanover
Marne
Claylick
Toboso
NEWARK
S.R. 657 ENDS HERE
S.R. 146 ENDS HERE
586
79
657
13
16
3

LOOP #15